Rave Reviews For

50 Biggest Website MISTAKES

In the past, I always cringed when people asked me to give them 'honest feedback' about their website. Because I knew I was going to see the same mistakes I always see—over and over. Now I can simply hand people a copy of this book and say, 'Use this as your checklist. When you've got all this covered, THEN come see me.' Do yourself a favor and buy at least 3 copies of this book. One for yourself, one for your webmaster, and one to give to a friend. It's that good!

Ray Edwards, Top Internet Copywriter
RayEdwards.com

When it comes to cranking things out on the Internet there are FEW people on the planet who measure up to the level the Frank Deardurff is at! He truly KNOWS what he's talking about and his book is filled with priceless info you MUST apply if you want to get incredible results online as well! Frank and his expertise come with my HIGHEST recommendation for sure!

Jason Oman
#1 Best-Selling Author of 'Conversations with Millionaires'
Featured TV Success Story on 'Creating Wealth' TV Infomercial
Author of 'Millionaire Money Formula'
Learn more about Jason at: http://JasonOman.com/AboutJason

"50 Biggest Website Mistakes" *is a must-have reference manual for all online business owners even IF you outsource all of your web design and development.*

This book serves as a checklist, reminder, and management tool to help you maintain control over all your projects and websites. Hand it off to new web designers and webmasters and make it required reading before doing any project. This way, you can literally turn over your websites and know that it's done RIGHT with the marketer's mindset!

Heather Seitz, EmailDelivered.com

In the medical world, people turn to specialists. In the online world, I turn to Frank and Bret. They are specialists and experts when it comes to your website.

Read this book, and be sure to implement each of their recommendations—your website and business will improve dramatically.

Dr. Kenny Handelman, addadhdblog.com

If there's anyone who should know about websites, it's Frank Deardurff—he has designed some of the most successful converting websites in Internet Marketing history, and continues to be two steps ahead of the game at all times. '50 Biggest Website Mistakes' is a crash course in the do's and don'ts of website marketing that you THINK you know already, until Frank proves how wrong you really are!

Don't assume ANYTHING—grab Frank's book TODAY, before you make a fatal marketing error!

"DJ" Dave Bernstein, www.HiFiWebGuy.com

The Book I should have written!

As someone that has been in the web design industry for over 16 years, I have to say I wish I had written this book and given it to every one of my clients before starting any project!

It's a great basic guide to all the things to do RIGHT with any website.

It doesn't matter if you have a current website or are just getting ready to build one, you MUST read this book and avoid a lot of mistakes I see every day.

Ely Delaney, MyBusinessMarketingMentor.com

> **"Mistakes are painful when they happen, but years later a collection of mistakes is what is called experience."**
>
> **– Denis Waitley**

50 Biggest Website MISTAKES

Secrets to Getting More Traffic, Converting More Customers, & Making More Sales

Bret Ridgway
& Frank Deardurff III

NEW YORK

50 BIGGEST WEBSITE MISTAKES

Secrets to Getting More Traffic, Converting More Customers, & Making More Sales

by Bret Ridgway & Frank Deardurff III

ISBN 978-1-60037-972-7 PB
ISBN 978-1-60037-973-4 EB
Library of Congress Control Number: 2011923753

Published by:

MORGAN JAMES PUBLISHING
The Entrepreneurial Publisher
5 Penn Plaza, 23rd Floor
New York City, New York 10001
(212) 655-5470 Office
(516) 908-4496 Fax
www.MorganJamesPublishing.com

Cover Design by:
Frank Deardurff III
frank@deardurff.com

Interior Design by:
Bonnie Bushman
bbushman@bresnan.net

In an effort to support local communities, raise awareness and funds, Morgan James Publishing donates one percent of all book sales for the life of each book to Habitat for Humanity.
Get involved today, visit
www.HelpHabitatForHumanity.org.

Dedications

To my wife Karen and my children Christina, Jacob and Mitchell. You are my reason why.

— **Bret Ridgway**

To my wife Sharon and my daughters Kellianne and Jessica, there aren't enough words to express what your love and support mean to me. To my grandchildren Logan and Amy, thanks for bringing a new magic into my heart. Always know that I love all of you, always and forever no matter what.

To my family and friends thanks for believing in me and for your continued support. Remember anything is possible.

— **Frank Deardurff III**

Sections

Foreword

Trust Me… I've seen it all. Having been online since 1996 I can tell you one thing. NOT all websites are equal when it comes to doing business on the Internet.

I've personally critiqued hundreds of business owner's sites over the past few years and I can tell you, without a doubt, there are SPECIFIC things you need to do in order to get the sale.

I've literally tested THOUSANDS of different combinations on my own sites and I can tell you, there are very specific changes you need to make to your websites in order to make them pull.

In their book, "The 50 Biggest Mistakes We See Online Business Owners Make", Bret Ridgway and Frank Deardurff have taken the guesswork out of it. They show you specific examples of what TO DO and what NOT TO DO.

If you are marketing online, YOU NEED THIS BOOK. It will save you a ton of money and time in avoiding mistakes and it will create incredible income by implementing their techniques. Don't wait get it right now.

This is a MUST HAVE READING!!!

—**Armand Morin**
http://ArmandMorin.com

Introduction

Online success is, to many, an oxymoron. It's as elusive as that greased pig at the county fair or the perfect wave for that surfer looking to catch the big one. For some, it's a pipe dream—something that other people get to realize but not something they'll ever achieve themselves.

Can Internet marketing be tricky? Sure. Will you have some failures as you strive to build your online business? Of course. But as some wise man once said — "If you're not failing at all that only means that you're not even trying anything." So keep your chin up—success might be just your next website away.

Online success is not one big thing. It's a bunch of little things that, when combined together and continually tweaked and improved, can lead to major successes. It's similar, in a sense, to the "Overnight Success" who spent twenty years perfecting his or her skills. To achieve online success you have to continuously add to your online skill set.

You've got in your hands one of those tools to help you add to your skill set. *50 Biggest Website Mistakes—The Biggest Mistakes We See Online Business Owners Make on Their Websites* takes a look at those critical factors that can spell the difference between an outright failure, a modest success, or an overwhelming success for a website.

We've taken what we've learned in our nearly 30 combined years of online experience and distilled it into quick, easy to digest nuggets of knowledge that you or your webmaster can apply almost immediately to your websites. The technical jargon is kept to a minimum and the explanations of what you should (and shouldn't) be doing on your websites are written from the perspective of the non-technical online business owner.

By avoiding these mistakes you will dramatically increase your chances of achieving online success. Now, it's a given that you need to find a hungry niche and provide them the products or services they want. But in today's ultra-competitive online world it's the little things you do that typically make the difference between your prospective customers purchasing from you or going to one of your competitors.

So, pay attention to these "little things" and watch your successes grow!

To your online success,

Bret Ridgway and *Frank Deardurff III*

Section #1

Your Visitor's Initial Impressions of Your Website

- Burying Your Key Information "Below the Fold"

- Trying to Do Too Much on One Site

- Not Accounting for Browser Differences

- Branding Boo Boos

- Did a Kid Do Your Site?

- Lost in the Background

- Color Me Successful

Biggest Website
MISTAKE #1

Burying Your Key Information "Below the Fold"

Most of us have probably heard the expression "Out of Sight, Out of Mind," which has many connotations for information marketers.

In Bret's earlier course *"The 50 Biggest Mistakes I See Information Marketers Make"* this expression was discussed in the context of how frequently you should make contact with your clients and prospective clients.

In the context of your website it can be applied to the information that is above and below the "fold". What do we mean by the fold? This old expression actually comes to us from newspapers. In the old days the "hottest" news was always placed in the top half of the newspaper, above the fold when your newspaper is folded in half.

Publishers recognized that on the newsstands they had to have the stories that would cause people to stop and read and buy their papers where it was readily visible. When you think about it, this still applies today.

On your website, the "fold" refers to the bottom edge of the viewable portion of your site when your homepage first loads. "Above the fold" is the part of your site that your visitors can see without scrolling down the page at all.

Here's one of Frank's websites—his blog at FrankDeardurff. com. What you see in the picture below is all the information that is "above the fold".

Obviously then, "below the fold" refers to any portion of a website page that your visitor must scroll down to view. That portion which is not visible in their browser window when your page loads.

You have only a scant few seconds to grab a visitor's attention. If you have information you believe is critical to drawing your reader in and getting them to continue to "consume" your website then you need to get that most critical information above the fold of your site, if at all possible.

Sometimes you may have a headline or header graphic (or both) that takes up a lot of the space above the "fold" of your website. In this scenario you may need to use a tool like a graphical arrow to direct people on down the page to a critical item, such as an optin box.

Any information below the "fold" of your website, is really "out of sight, out of mind" to your visitors. It's your challenge to make sure that the information that's "out of sight" doesn't remain invisible. Or you're in a serious world of hurt and your chances of getting your visitor to take the action you desire is seriously hampered.

Biggest Website MISTAKE #2

Trying to Do Too Much on One Site

We've seen it time and time again. You go to a website and everything is there, including the kitchen sink.

You've got outgoing links to recommended resources, you've got your recommended books on Amazon, you've got a compilation of articles, you've got a large product showcase, and seemingly everything else under the sun.

Speaking great John Childers once said, "A confused mind never buys." But a confused mind is exactly what you're creating when you offer too many options on a website.

Now it's okay to have a "corporate" or "catalog" site. But, if you're trying to sell a bunch of different products from this one site, and it's your only site, then you're probably overwhelming your visitor with too many options. They become confused and they leave, never to be seen again.

A general rule of thumb is one product, one website. This allows you to keyword optimize the page to draw traffic based on what you're selling on that particular page. If you have everything you offer on just one site it makes it very difficult to optimize that site for the search engines.

If you're using AdWords™ or some other pay-per-click search engine you should be driving traffic to a specific site that will do the sales job for you. If you send them to a corporate site you should at least send them directly to a subpage on the site that features the product you want to sell. Don't leave it to your visitor to search through your corporate or catalog site to find what you were advertising. Most won't do it unless they're really, really motivated.

Keep things simple for your visitors. One product—one site.

Biggest Website MISTAKE #3

Not Accounting for Browser Differences

It's so frustrating. You've worked your butt off creating a great looking website and you're sitting back admiring your handiwork.

You're so excited about your great new look and feel that you immediately upload your new site and make it live.

You bring up your new site in your browser and it looks just wonderful. You're so excited you call your friend up and ask him to take a look and the feedback is devastating.

According to your friend you've got text running into other areas, you have to scroll side to side to read the entire page and it looks like something a rank amateur would do. What happened?

There are a lot of different browsers out there these days, with everyone seemingly trying to create the "perfect" web browser for their needs or operating system. Just to clarify—a web browser is the application through which you view web pages.

This is an application that runs on your computer and, depending on your operating system, (Windows™, Apple™, Linux™ etc) determines what your default browser is.

Of course, you can change your default browser easily enough and there are many to choose from, the most common being Internet Explorer, Firefox, Safari, and Opera.

You're probably wondering why this makes a difference with your website. Well, fact is, that not all browser creators interpret your web page code exactly the same. Even though there is an organization called the W3 Consortium that has created a set of standards or guidelines each manufacturer interprets these in their own way or has their own preferences.

With these variations everything from your fonts, or any settings and widths can look different in each browser, as well as the same browser on a different operating system.

These differences can even change how your page functions. For example, we've seen instances where a form on a page in one browser works fine, where in another browser you can't even submit the form (click the button).

If you're adding any special coding to your website, such as using browser side scripting like JavaScript, it is even more important to cross check your pages in the different browsers just to make sure your code will function the way you want it to function. If you're using server side scripting such as PHP this is generally not an issue but it's always good to check.

You should also check the page on a few different computers and computer screens as well, because colors can vary, as well as what is viewable on the screen. To some this seems like overkill but imagine if your order page was the example above where the web visitor couldn't even click the submit button. There goes a sale.

Check Out Receipt

Ludington Library
610-525-1776
  www.lmls.org

Thursday, Nov 6 2014 7:06PM

Title: 50 biggest website mistakes : secrets to
getting more traffic, converting more customers,
& making more sales
Due: 11/28/2014

Title: The Facebook guide to small business mark
eting
Due: 11/28/2014

Title: Ultimate guide to Twitter for business :
generate quality leads using 140 characters, ins
tantly connect with 300 million customers in 10
minutes, discover 10 Twitter tools that can be a
polied now
Due: 11/28/2014

Total Items: 3

Thank you for using the Ludington Library. To
renew, call 610-525-1776 with card number or log
in at www.lmls.org. LMLS overdue fines: $3/day
for DVD,$.30/day for adult books, audiobooks and
music. $.20/day for children's books,audiobooks
and music.

Biggest Website
MISTAKE #4

Branding Boo Boos

One of the biggest mistakes we see with websites is a lack of identity, something that the visitor can recognize as your brand, whether it's a definable logo; tag line; or color theme. Be sure to carry that identifier through the whole sales process.

Too many times we see an optin page (the page a visitor comes to first when they visit your site and give you their name and email) that either was pretty basic or had one look and feel.

Then, after the visitor opts in, the page they're sent to has a different look and feel, only to be followed up by the shopping cart or order page that has yet a third different look and feel. This can create a total disconnect for your visitor.

In some cases it's hard to customize your shopping cart page to look exactly like your website. But, in most cases, you can upload or use a secure link for your logo. You can also customize some or all of the color settings to make those match your optin, sales and thank you pages.

Be sure to be consistent with your tag line or catch phrase as well. Also, the email address you use for communicating with your visitors is part of your branding.

While cleaning out an inbox recently email was sorted based on the "From" field and so many emails from the same marketers were totally inconsistent with their "from" line or even their email address.

Please understand we're not pointing fingers at all marketers, just stating the fact that we think some forget this rule. It's hard enough to get emails delivered consistently, so why make it more difficult by changing the way your name is formatted or the email address you use to send it from? There needs to be a certain identity carried through the whole process from the website and back to the website for follow-ups.

If you visit any of Frank's websites you will see some type of carry through to all of the sites. Most will have Frank's "That One" logo somewhere on the page and will either be Orange with Blue accent or Blue with Orange accent. And most, if not all, will have in the copyright section either "That One Corporation" or "That One Web Guy".

Also, when sending out email, autoresponders, newsletters or promotions all of my email comes from Frank – That One Web Guy! Unless it is from one of my joint ventures with a partner and we generally have a set email we use for communications for that partnership such as a support address or an info address.

Look around and you'll see branding all around you. There are certain companies you immediately recognize either because of the color, font or logo and you're immediately reassured this is a company you've learned to know, like, and trust over the lifetime of your relationship with that company.

You should follow the lead of the corporate giants. Even on a small scale this can be done. Think about your branding and stick with it.

Biggest Website
MISTAKE #5

Did a Kid Do Your Site?

This mistake is generally true to new website owners, but we've also seen it with people that have been online for awhile. That's a website that looks like you paid the next door neighbor's kid $20 to design for you.

It's true we've been told to get something up and then improve upon it. But, too many people stop at step one (put something up). Maybe some people get frozen by the technology when they're challenged with the task of either doing it themselves or finding someone capable of doing it for them.

It really doesn't have to be that difficult in any case. There are many places to locate free web page templates if you have to design the site yourself. All you need to do is go to your favorite search engine and enter in the search box "free web page templates". You'll be amazed at what you find.

One way to put up a website is to turn a WordPress blog into your sales page. The key here is to make sure it looks like a sales site and not a blog. There are a few WordPress templates available that will allow you to do just that.

For more information on how to put up a WordPress blog, along with a template you can use, visit WordPressStrategies.com

Another way to tackle getting up a website is to hire someone to do it. There are many resources out there, but many people don't know what questions to ask. So, if you visit 21WebmasterQuestions. com you can download a free report on what questions to ask a potential webmaster.

If you want to design it yourself you will want to be sure to make it clean and simple. Remember, in most cases, less is more. Keep it simple and test each element as you go. Test things such as your header graphic, website colors and even what fonts you use. Check out your competitors and see what they're doing.

If you're selling a product be sure to have the graphic components of the product match or compliment your website so they look like they go hand in hand.

Something that really stands out on a website that screams amateur is inconsistent fonts. Be sure to stick with the same font throughout. Also, be sure to have the website reviewed by friends and family and have it read and reread for typos and readability.

Following these tips will greatly improve the appearance of your website.

Here's one of the first sites ever developed by Bret, Pretty sad.

WELCOME TO MAINTENANCE RESOURCES TWI PRESS

Plant Engineering, Maintenance and Reliability Resource Site

Free Drawing
What's New
Reference Library
Events Calendar
PEM Links
Products Showcase
Bookstore
CMMS Connection
Discussion Forum
Free Magazines
On The Lighter Side
PEM Job-Line
Ordering Information
Contact Us

TWI Press is dedicated to providing plant engineering, maintenance and reliability professionals with a valuable on-line resource area. Here's what you'll find on this site.

FREE DRAWING - Just complete our on-line registration form and you'll be automatically entered in our monthly drawing for a free copy of the Rolling Bearings Troubleshooter's Guide on CD-ROM worth $297.

WHAT'S NEW? - If you're a regular visitor to our site then check here to see what's new to the site in the last 30 days.

REFERENCE LIBRARY - Need some technical info? TWI Press has put together a collection of free reference materials in our Reference Library. Look here for how-to articles, troubleshooting grids, and glossary of terms in many subject areas.

EVENTS CALENDAR - Want to know when the next plant engineering and maintenance show is going to be held? These events are great for checking out some of the newest plant engineering and maintenance products on the market and for learning more in the valuable conference sessions. You'll also find in this section a listing of available training courses in a wide variety of subjects.

PEM LINKS - Looking for other websites related to plant engineering and maintenance? Of course, you'll want to bookmark this TWI Press "Maintenance Resources" site. But to look at some more maintenance sites just click on PEM Links for a listing of and direct links to on-line trade journals, other reference sites, discussion/forum sites, commercial sites, and more.

PRODUCTS SHOWCASE - You don't have to search the heavens any longer for maintenance-related resource materials in CD-ROM format! You'll find a collection of CD-ROM resources for plant engineering, maintenance and reliability professionals, as well as other training courses, videotapes, books, job aids, and maintenance tools right here in the Products Showcase.

BOOKSTORE - Read a good book lately? You can find over one hundred books specially selected for plant engineering and maintenance personnel in our Bookstore. From electronics to hydraulics, from maintenance management to HVAC, from welding to Total Productive Maintenance, you'll find it here.

CMMS CONNECTION - This on-line resource links you directly to most of the primary Computerized Maintenance Management Software providers. If you're looking for a CMMS package this may be just the place to start.

FREE MAGAZINES - By special arrangement with the publishers you can order free trial issues or subscriptions to several leading plant engineering and maintenance related magazines or newsletters by completing one on-line form.

LIGHTER SIDE - When you need a short break from the seriousness of your day check out the Lighter Side. Updated weekly.

PEM JOB-LINE - If you're a company looking for plant engineering, maintenance or reliability professionals, or a professional looking for a new position check into the PEM Job-Line.

We hope you'll enjoy your visit to the TWI Press "Maintenance Resources" website. Please register so you can be kept apprised of new additions to this site. Site registrants are also eligible for valuable prize drawings. See the registration form for this month's reward. Thanks for visiting!

Registration	What's New	Library	Events	Links
Products	Bookstore	CMMS	To Order	Contact Us
Discussion	Subscription	HOME	Lighter Side	Job-Line

TWI Press can be reached by

Phone: 812.232.0753
Fax: 812.232.3978
E-Mail: info@maintenanceresources.com
Via Mail: 120 South 7th Street
Terre Haute, IN 47807

Biggest Website MISTAKE #6

Lost in the Background

This common mistake is seen on lots of websites. It seems to go in phases but it's still happening quite a bit. This mistake is that the website background is WAY too busy.

Most commonly seen is the "logo background". That's where the logo is rotated 45° and repeated to create a background pattern. Not only does this look outdated, it also distracts the visitor's focus from the webpage.

Many times you see a wild pattern or color that is way too bright and again, this takes the focus away from the content on the website.

Of course, this problem isn't only with the web page background, but also on table backgrounds on the webpage itself. Many times the background colors or patterns for the testimonials are too dark or busy and make it hard to read. Other areas you might use backgrounds are places such as your guarantee, order area, bonus description, and product description.

When designing your web page in these areas always remember less is more. Use simple muted colors that enhance or compliment the design elements on the page. Dark colors only work for certain niches but remember too much reverse text makes it very hard to read for long periods. Reverse text is where you have a black or very dark background color and white text on top for the content.

Being lost in the background can also be the complete opposite of what we've discussed already. What we mean is by not having any background or some sort of "edges" to the webpage to help keep the readers eye moving down the webpage.

The same is true for the other areas we mentioned such as the guarantee and order boxes. By not having any type of background or "container" your offer or focus is lost and blends into the background or mixes right in with the regular copy of the website and loses its purpose for even being on the page.

So, next time when you're designing or redesigning your web pages remember to keep the focus on the areas that make you the money and to accentuate, not distract from the task at hand.

Biggest Website
MISTAKE #7

Color Me Successful

One of the single most overlooked areas in marketing is the use of color on websites and in offline marketing pieces.

The way we view colors psychologically triggers how we feel, think, or even buy.

Colors are similar to words as they both have interpretations as to their meanings. Are you stirring the right emotions with your online and offline marketing? Marketing pieces such as your website, newsletter, company logo or business card could be sending the wrong message without you even knowing it!

With the cost of print materials ever changing you want to make sure you get it right before you go to press, checking and rechecking spelling, grammatical errors, names, slogans and more; but overlooking the message you are conveying with the color.

On the web we can (and should) test and modify regularly, and we are taught to change headlines and sub-headlines and rephrase paragraphs or move pictures but how many of us actually test the colors of our headlines or backgrounds and borders?

The following are frequently used colors and the definition of how these colors are perceived.

BLACK—suggests authority, power, boldness, seriousness, is distinguishing and classic. Business wise it's great for creating drama and is good for a background color (except on websites, it's very hard on the eyes). It's ideal for text on a light background. Black also implies submission and is associated with evil.

BLUE – represents trust and suggests security, authority, faithfulness and dignity. For business it suggests sanctuary and fiscal responsibility. It is the most popular and the second most powerful color.

Blue can also represent solitude, sadness, depression, wisdom, trust and loyalty. It is associated to ice and cold. Studies have shown that people are more productive in blue rooms. Research also shows that people retain more information after reading text written in blue. Good tip for headlines in web copy.

BABY BLUE—suggests weakness.

BROWN—suggests richness, politeness, helpfulness and effectiveness. In business it suggests less important items.

Brown is generally a favorite color for men. Solid, reliable brown is the color of earth and is abundant in nature. Light brown implies genuineness while dark brown is similar to wood or leather. It communicates credibility, solidity, strength and maturity.

GOLD – suggests wealth.

GRAY—suggests authority, practicality, earnestness and creativity. Business wise it is traditional and conservative.

GREEN – is the color of nature and suggests health, fertility, freedom, freshness, healing, tranquility and jealousy. Businesses use it to communicate status and wealth. It is the easiest color on the eye and can improve vision. It is a calming, refreshing color.

ORANGE—is associated with warmth, contentment, and wholesomeness. It suggests pleasure, excitement, cheer, endurance, strength generosity and ambition.

For business it is good for highlighting information on charts and graphs. It can be used to indicate that a product is suitable for everyone, and can make an expensive product seem more affordable.

PINK—represents femininity, gentleness, well being and innocence. For business you must be aware of its feminine links and implications.

PURPLE—suggests spirituality, royalty, luxury, wealth, sophistication, authority and mournfulness. It is also feminine and romantic. However, because it is rare in nature, purple can appear artificial.

RED—symbolizes heat, fire, blood, love, warmth, power, excitement, strength, sex, passion, vitality, risk, danger, aggressiveness and commands attention. Words and objects in red get people's attention immediately. Financially it is associated with debt, it is great for boldness and accents. The most emotionally intense color, red stimulates a faster pulse and breathing. The color red is extremely overpowering and it's recommended to be used as an accent and not as a background.

WHITE – is the color of innocence and purity. It is most used as a background color but can also be used to accentuate or highlight a darker color. Most associate white with things that are clean and sterile. It is also used to represent cold, cool and refreshing.

YELLOW – is a spiritual color and symbolizes the deity in many religions. Bright yellow can be tiring and irritable to the eye when used in large quantities. Yellow is similar to the color red as it speeds metabolism. It is often used to highlight or draw attention and represents caution. A softer yellow is related to the color of warmth and happiness.

When designing a company logo or brand it makes sense to use color to establish an image or perceived image based on the "definition" of that color. Use of color in branding is simply common sense marketing.

Take a second to think about some of the top brands to see if they have done the same. When you think of Coca-Cola™ do you see red? With Tide™ detergent you automatically think of the color Orange. Ford™ blue; McDonald's ™ "Golden" Arches; you could go on and on with the color association but the biggest point do you think it was just a fluke they picked those colors?

My personal opinion is that they studied their market, researched the locations they would be selling in to determine what colors are interpreted which ways.

You could easily do the same thing with some simple marketing research of your own. By observing other marketing efforts in the locations you will be selling to which could be time consuming if you do not live in that area or are planning on promoting worldwide.

An Ask Campaign using the Ask Database™ is even a simpler method of conducting marketing research right from the comfort of your home or office. Find it online at AskDatabase.com.

When designing your website you have to think about your audience and what your objectives are for your site. What colors will best help you accomplish your goals?

Section #2

Improving Readability of Your Website

- Fooling Around with Fonts

- Not Maximizing Your Headlines

- Intimidating Paragraphs

- Typos in Copy and Code

- Columns Too Wide

Biggest Website MISTAKE #8

Fooling Around with Fonts

Sometimes it's difficult for a website designer to resist getting carried away with their use of fonts. Maybe that website designer is YOU. In the world of websites usage of fonts is an area where it's definitely a case of less is more. Just pick one or two fonts of the same style and stick with it.

But what do we mean by "style"? In fonts there are what are called "Serif Fonts" and what are called "Sans Serif Fonts". A "serif" is a non-structural detail on the end of some of the strokes that make up letters and symbols.

You and I might refer to them as "fancy" letters. For printed materials most studies show that Serif fonts are best for readability.

Commonly used "Serif" fonts are:

Times New Roman
Georgia
Courier

The word "sans" means "without". So "Sans Serif" fonts are those that do not have the extra brush stroke at the end of each character. You and I might refer to these as "plain" letters.

Three of the more commonly used "Sans Serif" fonts are:

Arial
Tahoma
Verdana

On the web readability is the complete opposite. Testing has proven that Sans Serif fonts are much easier to read online. Most successful marketers prefer Tahoma font for headlines and subheads. Those same marketers typically utilize Arial font for body copy and navigation.

There are a few cases where crossing the style border is acceptable. An example is if you are adding testimonials or case studies to your webpage. If you want to differentiate between the main copy and the special callout of a testimonial or case study then an alternate font type is acceptable for that testimonial or case study.

Certainly, you should be consistent throughout all of your testimonials to utilize the same font style for each, same for case studies.

That all being said, the key to online success is testing, testing, testing. Only your readers can tell you with any certainty what will work best for them. Maybe you have a freakish niche that responds best to something different than the norm. But, always start with the norm and test variations from there.

Biggest Website MISTAKE #9

Not Maximizing Your Headlines

Headlines and sub headlines is an area where many Internet marketers kinda, sorta do it correctly. But, they still miss an important step to make the MOST out of them.

What are headlines and sub headlines? Headlines are found at the top of a web page, mostly on the optin and sales letter pages. They generally use a larger font size then the body copy and almost always are boldfaced.

Sub headlines (or subheads) are found throughout the sales page and should be slightly smaller than the main headlines. Generally, subheads use a different font color than the headline and are also bolded.

A common rule of thumb is to make the headline 4 font sizes bigger than the body copy and the subheads 2 sizes bigger than the body copy. For example, if your body copy is 12 point type than your headlines should be at least 16 point type and your subheads should be 14 point. Sometimes it may be acceptable to go a little larger on the headlines and subheads. As always, testing is the key.

A couple of things in the headline itself that often gets overlooked is changing the color of action words in the headline and adding quotes to the headline. It's been proven that headlines get a higher conversion if you add " at the beginning of and " at the end of the headlines. This is a simple thing to do and well worth it.

The other overlooked point is that when creating your headline you will want to emphasize particular action words in your headline.

For example, in the following headline …

"Learn the Hidden Secrets to Writing Award Winning Headlines by Using the Same Strategies Top Internet Marketers Use!"

I would emphasize the words "Hidden Secrets" and "Top Internet Marketers Use" as shown below.

"Learn the Hidden Secrets to Writing Award Winning Headlines by Using the Same Strategies Top Internet Marketers Use!"

Generally, if you bold two separate parts of the same headline you should make it where the two emphasized parts, when read together, make sense. In this example the bolded text catches your eye and if you only read the text emphasized in red it says "Hidden Secrets Top Internet Marketers Use!" If you only wanted to bold one section you might test bolding "Award Winning Headlines".

A great resource tool for headline writing is Carl Galletti's "2001 Greatest Headlines Ever Written." You'll find this publication available at: http://marketingclassics.com/2001headlines.htm

Subheads are generally shorter so the practice of emphasizing more than one segment of an individual headline generally doesn't apply. However, you need to take the same consideration with subheads as you do with the headline. You want your headline compelling enough to grab the visitor's attention and get them to read the first line of your sales letter and so on.

You want your subheads to compel your reader to continue on through your sales letter. In fact, you want your subheads to, in essence, be kind of a mini sales letter in itself. Many people simply scan sales letters. They're going to scan your sales letter by reading the headline and subheads. The reader should be able to understand the crux of your sales letter simply by reading your subheads.

That's why you want to avoid subheads that are too simple. An example that you'll find of a subhead on many sites is something like…

"Here's Why!"

Now, how compelling is that? Here's why what? Yeah, you might get someone that is intrigued and would want to know what the "why" is. But, you can get the benefits of both a higher keyword count and a more intriguing subhead if you do something like…

"Here's Why a Headline Swipe File is a No Brainer"

Isn't that more compelling? Now, wouldn't you want to read more? Plus, if your product is about headlines you've added more relevance to your keyword count.

Biggest Website MISTAKE #10

Intimidating Paragraphs

Let's say someone comes to visit your website and they see a big block of text such as you see in Example One below.

— Example One —

Lorem ipsum dolor sit amet, consectetuer adipiscing elit. Sed quis ante. Suspendisse potenti. Nunc sed lorem non velit viverra imperdiet. Morbi leo. Pellentesque rhoncus, massa at condimentum mollis, ligula lorem malesuada libero, non suscipit lorem massa in sapien. Praesent vitae neque non urna tempus consequat. Quisque scelerisque mi sit amet tellus. Donec sodales lorem quis nunc. Donec sit amet enim. Donec facilisis mi sed lorem. Cras odio felis, vehicula sed, pharetra et, egestas non, pede. Pellentesque faucibus arcu quis metus elementum volutpat. Sed lorem tellus, lacinia et, pulvinar at, porttitor id, ipsum. Maecenas eros. Nulla orci. Vivamus et lacus. Mauris tellus. Quisque felis libero, gravida facilisis, fermentum ac, mattis et, metus. Suspendisse at sapien. Vestibulum vel sapien.

Donec gravida, leo et ultricies lobortis, nisi felis hendrerit nulla, vitae interdum massa turpis non justo. Sed nec elit ac ipsum porttitor mattis. Maecenas at metus. Ut dictum, erat sit amet egestas consequat, risus lorem posuere odio, a pretium felis dui nec massa. Vestibulum sollicitudin lectus at odio viverra mattis. Integer nisl. In sed pede. Suspendisse laoreet, tortor dapibus bibendum commodo, nunc urna aliquam odio, in bibendum lectus tortor eu quam. Donec egestas feugiat lectus. Suspendisse potenti. Ut malesuada condimentum justo. Fusce vel nulla non dolor commodo mattis. Duis eget libero volutpat urna tristique elementum. Proin luctus. Morbi in nisl. Fusce condimentum diam in lorem. Mauris hendrerit.

— End Example One —

Here's the typical reaction – "Ugh, I've got to read all that? I'm not going to do that." So they click off your site and are gone forever. Those large blocks of text are simply too intimidating for your visitor and their choice will be to not read what you've written.

So what should you do?

What you should do is what's called "paragraph chunking". Take your big paragraphs and break them into smaller chunks—no more than 4 to 5 lines total per paragraph.

You'll find that by applying this technique to your web page it will appear there isn't as much to read even though there is a page full of text. Your visitor won't be overwhelmed by seeing a plethora of text and leave your site.

In this next example we how the same text in Example One would look "chunked".

— Example Two —

Lorem ipsum dolor sit amet, consectetuer adipiscing elit. Sed quis ante. Suspendisse potenti. Nunc sed lorem non velit viverra imperdiet. Morbi leo. Pellentesque rhoncus, massa at condimentum mollis, ligula lorem malesuada libero, non suscipit lorem massa in sapien. Praesent vitae neque non urna tempus consequat. Quisque scelerisque mi sit amet tellus.

Donec sodales lorem quis nunc. Donec sit amet enim. Donec facilisis mi sed lorem. Cras odio felis, vehicula sed, pharetra et, egestas non, pede. Pellentesque faucibus arcu quis metus elementum volutpat. Sed lorem tellus, lacinia et, pulvinar at, porttitor id, ipsum. Maecenas eros. Nulla orci. Vivamus et lacus. Mauris tellus.

Quisque felis libero, gravida facilisis, fermentum ac, mattis et, metus. Suspendisse at sapien. Vestibulum vel sapien. Donec gravida, leo et ultricies lobortis, nisi felis hendrerit nulla, vitae interdum massa turpis non justo. Sed nec elit ac ipsum porttitor mattis.

Maecenas at metus. Ut dictum, erat sit amet egestas consequat, risus lorem posuere odio, a pretium felis dui nec massa. Vestibulum sollicitudin lectus at odio viverra mattis. Integer nisl. In sed pede. Suspendisse laoreet, tortor dapibus bibendum commodo, nunc urna aliquam odio, in bibendum lectus tortor eu quam. Donec egestas feugiat lectus.

Suspendisse potenti. Ut malesuada condimentum justo. Fusce vel nulla non dolor commodo mattis. Duis eget libero volutpat urna tristique elementum. Proin luctus. Morbi in nisl. Fusce condimentum diam in lorem. Mauris hendrerit.

— End Example Two —

In Example Two you have the same amount of text, but because it's broken into five paragraphs rather than two it appears much easier to read.

One thing to remember when breaking apart the paragraphs is to not break the text where you would have a single word on a line by itself. Reword the paragraph slightly or push another word or two down from the previous line to give you a better look.

Biggest Website MISTAKE #11

Typos in Copy and Code

Typos or typographical errors are common since the beginning of the written word and, of course, misspoken words as well.

But on a website or printed marketing ad this can be very costly. In a quick search on the Internet we found some famous typos and their ramifications (these were found at typobuddy.com)

"In July 2007 A Roswell, New Mexico-based car dealership sent out 50,000 scratch-off ads each as $1000.00 winners. Touting a grand prize of $1,000 (which was to be 1 in 50,000), these cards were incorrectly printed by an Atlanta-based Force Events Direct Marketing Co. The result was 50,000 crazed locals who thought they had each won the grand prize, calling the dealership to cash-in. Realizing that a $50,000,000 pay-off was neither intended or realistic, this unnamed dealership has offered to hand out $5 Wal-Mart gift cards in exchange for the misprinted scratchers, which equaled a paltry $250,000. Additionally, Force Events held a $5,000 drawing for anyone with a ticket, in an attempt to quell the immediate dissatisfaction of the townspeople, as well as a series of 20 other drawings— each with a $1,000 prize."

———

"In September 2006, A trader at Mizuho Securities accidentally sold 610,000 shares in J-Com Co. (a job recruiting company) for 1 yen a piece, instead of 1 share at 610,000 yen. Unable to cancel the order Mizuho Securities has lost roughly $340 million as a result. Just think how lucky you would have been to purchase a few pieces of this stock! Attributed to "fat-finger" syndrome, which is stock trader slang for making large blunders, the trader's name has not been made public (likely for security purposes). When Mizuho contacted the Tokyo Stock Exchange, the latter cited a glitch in its system that made this trade irrevocable. Discussions have occurred with the possibility of Mizuho and the TSE somehow sharing the loss, but still no agreement has been reached."

———

"A Student at Stanford University, Sean Anderson, accidentally helped Larry Page come up with the name and spelling of Google. While Page and Anderson were in Page's office, the two were attempting to come up for a name for the would-be search behemoth. Sean had suggested verbally the word "googolplex", spurning Page to shorten it to "googol". Anderson then went to check the availability of the word, accidentally spelling it "Google" in an internet domain name registry. Available it was, and the company has decided to go with this spelling ever since. Whether or not the company has succeeded because of the name is subject to some speculation, it is very interesting to see what has become of a basic spelling error. It also goes to show that not all typos result in lives being ruined and/or financial turmoil, way to go Sean Anderson (although he now works for Microsoft)."

———

Obviously, it is a good idea to check and recheck your website copy, newsletter content and marketing pieces before releasing to the Internet. If at all possible, have someone else reread the copy before publishing it live.

The same goes for programming code for your website.

Simple typos can cause ill effects or hours of recoding because of one keystroke or missed punctuation. A rule of thumb is if you've entered code in the html of your website and it isn't working quite right, and you've spent considerable time trying to figure out where the code is broken, then have a friend or another person with code experience look at it.

You would not believe the number of times a period has been inserted in code instead of a comma or an accent mark instead of an apostrophe or simply a colon was missed at the end of a statement.

Biggest Website MISTAKE #12

Columns Too Wide

A common problem with websites today is column widths that seem to be growing right along with monitor sizes. Just because the monitor sizes are bigger doesn't mean your website copy should be.

We imagine there will be some changes as monitor sizes grow but a good rule of thumb is that your sales page should be no wider than about 760 pixels, with 1000 pixels being the topside limit. It is imperative to be fully aware of your website visitor's monitor size for your niche market.

This is really easy to check with stats packages that you may already have on your website. With many web-hosting packages today you have access to a web stats package called AWstats™. If your web host doesn't offer this you can easily incorporate Google Analytics™ into your website. Both of these stats packages have details about your visitor's browser settings and screen resolution, so be sure to keep that in mind when laying out your website and adjust accordingly.

Be sure to take every precaution not to have a horizontal scroll bar showing that makes your visitor scroll left to right to view your full page. Keep your sales page at least 20 pixels smaller than your average visitor's screen resolution. For example, if your average visitor has the screen resolution of 1024x768 (this is the most common) then you want to set your sales page to 1000 pixels or less.

760 to 800 pixels is a good width for readability. Even with your page size set to either of those widths you will want to have between a 15 and 20 pixel margin on the left and right hand sides of the page. By applying these settings it gives you a good visual appeal and with the wider "gutter" on the sides it gives the eyes an easy path to flow down through the copy.

You see the similar margins in print materials for obvious reasons. So there's no reason we shouldn't continue with these proven methods on our web pages.

Another thing to consider if you are planning to have your pages printed out is to set your page and margins so that your copy is 600 pixels wide. That is the width that transfers over to a standard printed page.

There are web technologies now in place that will format your wider page to the narrower page for print automatically when the visitor selects print in the file menu of the browser. If you are interested in learning about this technology, be sure to search for "CSS Media Type Print." You can also learn more about these settings and more in Frank's course Web Page Secrets Revealed.

Here's a screen shot of one of Bret's sites with the screen resolution set at 1024 x 768.

Below is the same website with the screen resolution set at 800 x 600.

Usability Issues Your Visitors Face

- Help with Hyperlinks

- Navigation Nightmares

- Order Page Out of Order

- Broken Links

- Order Buttons

Help with Hyperlinks

This website mistake has been an issue for a long time but with some of the newer technologies that have been introduced it's only gotten easier to make this mistake.

What we're talking about are hyperlinks.
A hyperlink is a section of text that has been given some code instruction to go to a different location, either on the page or to a different website all together when someone clicks on it.

The biggest problem we see is that many website owners or webmasters try to change the appearance of a hyperlink—either to make it "blend" with the site or to hide the fact it's a link at all.

The best analogy we can think of to describe why this is important is this. "If it looks like a duck, sounds like a duck, and walks like a duck, then it must be a duck!"

Think about this—if it looks like a hyperlink and responds like a hyperlink, then it must be a hyperlink. Too many times people have added styles to the link to make it appear a different color or added coding to make the underline disappear. Plus add a lot of underlined text in their sales copy that confuses people as to where the links actually are.

Remember a confused shopper rarely buys. They just stay confused and then leave. **<u>A hyperlink should always remain blue and underlined</u>**. If you are going to add ANY programming to a hyperlink it would be to enable a rollover action.

What a rollover does is when the website visitor places their mouse over the link it changes color. I generally like to use red for this action because it catches the visitor's eye. By adding this rollover or hover action it lets them know something is about to happen and verifies the fact that it is actually a link and not just underlined text.

Some conversion specialists will even tell you that you'll get a higher conversion rate by leaving the link blue, adding the rollover or hover over action AND applying some code to change the cursor to the pointer finger.

The ONLY place where you might want to disable the appearance of a hyperlink is in spots where you really don't want them to click, but need to have the link on the page. You're probably wondering why you would even include such a link on the page.

It is always a good idea to have footer navigation on the page for things like your earnings disclaimer; privacy policy; support links and even a link to a site map for search engine spidering. Obviously, these are needed but you really don't want the visitor to click on these, you only want them to click on the order links. So for this section you can add a style to set decoration = to none. That will remove the underline but I would ONLY use that tip for the footer section.

Another thing about hyperlinks is that many website owners don't include enough buy links on their page. On way too many sites you have to hunt for the link to buy the product. Remember, you generally have less than 10 seconds to get a visitor's attention. If they have to hunt for your order links they will move on and hunt for another site that will take their money.

You want to be sure to have anywhere from 9 to 12 links on your sales page asking for the sale and not just, "click here to order now". Be a little creative; add keywords or actions words like, "Click here to learn about using Hyperlinks"

Finally, hyperlinks should not really link to another site off your sales page. Obviously, if you link away from your site there's a good chance they won't return. BUT, if you must link to something off your site make sure that link opens in a new window. You can do this by adding a target= "_blank" to your URL.

For example, that would look like the following:

```
<a href="http://www.that1domain.com"
target="blank">Click Here</a>
```

Biggest Website MISTAKE #14

Navigation Nightmares

There are many types of navigation that can be used on a website and many locations on a page that navigation can be placed. Obviously, too many locations can be a problem because the website visitor can easily get distracted from the primary objective of your website or just frustrated because they can't easily figure out where to go first.

Simplicity is generally best.

When setting up your navigation structure for your menus think about simplicity. If you can explain what the link is in one or two words that will be best. Nothing is more confusing than a menu button with two lines of text, plus it breaks up uniformity.

Also, decide which location works the best for simplicity. Many times you find navigation either on the left or right sides of the page AND along the top under the header graphic. Ideally you want to stick to one location. Obviously, a menu across the top is limited to the width of your page where as a menu down one side or the other will give you more options. And, of course, you wouldn't want two rows of buttons across the top.

Something else you want to consider when creating your navigation links is to make sure you use colors and fonts that are readable. This can be easily achieved without becoming overbearing. Be sure to create some sort of "action" when the visitor places their mouse over the button or link. This can be accomplished by using either what is called a rollover graphic or an "on mouse over" text action.

This gives the visitor confirmation that something is going to happen when they click the link. Ideally, if you are working on a single page sales letter site you don't want any navigation, at least in the form of buttons.

Obviously you will need some navigation links on your sales page and the best place for those is in the footer section of the page. Again simplicity rules, you only need a few key links when creating the single page sales letter. You'll want items such as your privacy policy; disclaimer, support link and maybe even an order now link.

One other form of navigation links on a single page sales letter page is what are called "jump links" or anchor tags. This strategy allows you to "jump" down the sales page to a predefined anchor point.

For example, if you have order links on your sales page it has been proven that you get better conversions if you link those order links to an order area of your sales page. That way your visitor can see your complete offer and bonuses. This is done using the anchor link technique.

You can also create sales letters where the sales letter starts off with a bulleted list of action items which link to strategic points in the sales letter such as: frequently asked questions and testimonials.

As you can see, there are a lot of things to consider when creating the navigation strategy for your website.

Biggest Website MISTAKE #15

Order Page Out of Order

A quick way to lose a hard earned sale is to have an order page that is out of sync with the rest of your website.

We're told time and time again that people buy from those they know, like and trust. We do everything we can on the optin page to get that first sign of acceptance from them to opt-in.

We add more techniques on the sales page to build further on the trust and let the visitor know who we are. Then we blow it by not having a cohesive look and feel to our order page.

To clarify, we have a template or design on our optin page and sales page that matches in color, as well as the header matching on both of those pages but then we get to the cart page or better known as the order page and it looks nothing like the other pages.

So many times the order page is left completely as plain as the shopping cart service built it. Now, it's true that some cart services won't allow much customization. Almost all of them will allow some sort of modification if you look in their settings.

Some services will only allow you to upload your logo, which will at least allow you to carry over some similarity to your existing site. You will need to be cautious and make sure that if the cart allows you to upload an image make sure that they are uploading to their secure server or you utilize a service such as SecureWebImages.com that will host your logo for you on a secure server.

If your image is not secure your visitors will see a warning message saying that some elements on the page are not secure and will ask them if they want to proceed.

In most cases they will just leave and not continue with their order. Also the same will happen if they are unsure if they are on the right order page for your product.

If they are uncertain that they are on the right page they will surely hesitate to place the order.

Biggest Website MISTAKE #16

Broken Links

Obviously this can be a major problem on your website and we've seen it happen time and time again. It's actually pretty common as well as an easy thing to have happen to you. Just to clarify, what we're talking about are broken hyperlinks on your website.

A broken link can happen due to many different factors such as, typos, deleted files, or bad URLs. Also, something to consider is what type of server your website is hosted on.

One thing that many website owners are not aware of is that some server operating systems make filenames and folder names case sensitive.

If your web hosting is on a Windows™ based server a filename is not case sensitive, meaning that a file named contactus.htm and ContactUs.htm would be looked at as the same file. But, on a Linux™ based server they would appear as two different files.

The same is true with folders, as a Windows™ server would see the folder named images and Images as the same folder where as a Linux™ based server would see them as two different folders.

Something else to be aware of is the common problem of leaving spaces in between two words in a filename. If you were to have a file with the file name of contact us.htm many times the URL would get transformed to contact%20us.htm which of course would cause a broken link.

A good way to keep from getting typos in the URL would be to browse the correct link and then copy and paste that URL when creating the hyperlink.

A good habit to get into when creating any type of link on your web page is to test the link after uploading the page. This is also true when creating web forms and order links that have thank you URLs or redirect URLs.

Be sure to fill out the form and see that you land on the page you expected as well as placing a test order to make sure you reach the thank you page that you have put into place.

A broken link can cost you leads, or even worse lost revenue from missed sales.

Biggest Website MISTAKE #17

Order Buttons

We see this mistake quite a bit or maybe we don't! So many times we see order buttons and form submit buttons that don't appear to be buttons.

Many web designers will make great looking graphical buttons to "match" the design of the rest of the site. While these buttons might look nice they aren't always effective.

Order Now

There has been a lot of debate about whether graphical buttons are as effective as regular "HTML" style buttons. We suggest you test what works best for your market, but we'll make the comment you may have heard before—if it looks like a button and acts like a button then it must be a button.

Click Here To Order Today! »

Why would you want to chance the possibility of lost sales by "hoping" the website visitors realize that the graphic button you have in place is perceived is a button?

This goes the same for your opt-in form buttons. You should be consistent with the buttons so the visitor knows what is and isn't a button.

There are a few things you can do to "enhance" the regular "HTML" button to improve your results. You can see an example of some these effects by visiting 50BiggestWebsiteMistakes.com. You can see we've increased the size of the button and text as well as adding a red border around the button to help draw attention to the button. This increases action to the button.

Just as is true with many elements of marketing, copy is king, even on something as small as a button. By default the text on a HTML button says simply "submit", which really doesn't say much. You want to change the text or copy on the button to have some sort of instruction or action so that there is no question what's going to happen when they push the button.

Some examples of copy to use on an order button would be "Click Here To Order Now"; "Order Now for Only $29.95". A few examples for the opt-in button would be "Claim Your Report Today!" or "Get A Free Chapter!".

By applying several of these strategies just with the button itself you'll be surprised how much you will improve conversion of opt-ins and orders. Of course, be sure that you test everything and monitor by using your stats programs.

"If you cannot measure it, you can not improve it"

– Lord Kelvin

Looking at Your Visitor's Overall Experience

- Where are Your Autoresponders?

- Lack of Audio

- Stale Content

- Not Very Beneficial

- Upsell Utopia or Upsell Hell

- You Call This Support?

Biggest Website MISTAKE #18

Where are Your Autoresponders?

This is a common mistake made by both new and veteran website owners. And that is either no or not enough follow up autoresponders.

First, let's explain what an autoresponder is. In most cases an autoresponder is an email message that is automatically sent in reply when someone sends an email to that account. This can be triggered either directly by email or via a web form.

In marketing we use the word autoresponder to refer to sequential autoresponders, meaning that after someone triggers a response they receive a series of messages sent over time. This is also known as an email follow up series.

How and why you would want to use an autoresponder on your website. First—the how. Someone comes to your website and you have a spot on your website where they fill in their name and email to receive more information from you such as a free report, a free chapter or even a sample video of your product.

When they give you that information you send them an email automatically with the information they requested or information about how they can claim their promised information.

Here's where the problem comes in. Generally, many marketers or website owners get in a hurry and insert that first message, intending to go back and add more later. But they forget all about it.

Now the why. In sending that email message you are starting a relationship with that prospective customer. This is important because, in most cases, website visitors are on your website for only a short period of time before they are off to find out what other info they can gather about that topic.

So, by creating a follow up autoresponder you can send them not only the promised information but every two or three days you can follow up with them with more information about the product that will hopefully entice them to ultimately buy your product.

Obviously the number of "touches" it takes varies on every niche market and is also determined by the price. In most cases, the higher the price the more connections you may need to make.

With most autoresponder services you can discontinue this autoresponder series after the prospect becomes a client, which of course is the smart thing to do because you don't want to keep sending presale messages if they've already purchased.

But what now you may ask? Well, you will want to start a post sales autoresponder message, and this is where many marketers drop the ball. In your post autoresponder messages you want to teach them how to get the most out of your product they just bought.

Why? Because it makes them a happy customer if they actually see results from your product or service. Many times someone will buy a product and then not follow through and actually use it to its fullest and then question you because they didn't.

If you create follow up emails after the purchase leading them through your book; course; or services then they are more than likely going to buy the follow up product or additional products from you as you release them, which of course you can add into your follow up emails.

That's why it's important to get both the pre and post autoresponders into place before you launch a product or get them in place shortly after so you will see more conversion—both pre and post sales.

And if you've hired a copywriter for your sales copy many of them will include the autoresponders at an additional price for you. Just be sure to ask and let them know the number of responders you need.

Biggest Website MISTAKE #19

Lack of Audio

It's been proven that people learn or process information in different ways. Some people are visual learners while others are auditory. It's a good idea to cover all bases when creating your websites.

In website testing we've seen a major conversion increase when we add audio to our web pages. By adding audio to various places on our websites we help those who learn through auditory instruction consume the page. Even website visitors that are visual learners like the audio bites that we add. It enhances the overall experience and they tend to consume more of the whole process.

Here are some ways that you should add audio to your website. First off, when using an optin page it's always a good idea to include an audio on that page. Be sure to leave a brief pause at the beginning so that you don't startle the visitor with a sudden blast of sound. This will cause them to leave the site quicker than anything.

- Other places to utilize audio on your website include:
- Welcome message on the sales page

- Testimonials

- About you

- The guarantee

- Product description

- Exit survey asking them why they left without buying

- Order page telling them what to fill in or where they'll find the order button

- Describing upsells or bonuses

The final place in the whole sales process is to have an audio on the thank you page. Confirm that their order was placed and maybe explain to the visitor how to sign up for your newsletter or instructions on how to locate your blog.

For the most part, we as website owners think most of the process is logical. But we shouldn't take it for granted that our website visitors will understand the path we have put in place for them.

So, the guided audio messages will welcome, explain, convince and confirm their experience with you as a website owner and in the end allow you to create more sales time after time.

Biggest Website MISTAKE #20

Stale Content

This mistake happens more so with website owners that have multiple sites than those that have just one or two but it happens to just about any website owner at some point or another.

What we're talking about is stale or old content on the site.

A definition of stale would be:

Not fresh; musty; stagnant; having lost novelty or interest; having lost freshness, having lost force or effectiveness through absence of action, as a claim.

Any website can easily become any one of these things over time and, in some niche markets, even faster than others. Certain markets obviously have longer "shelf" life as the content is tried and true and works time after time. But, in other technological areas, information changes so rapidly that we need to update the content to make it relevant to the current standards.

Not only does the content tend to get stale but also does the look and feel. The design may have been state of the art 5 years ago but as you surf the web you can tell the sites that are new and the ones that have been around a while. Some visitors will take one look at the site and assume that the content must be old and irrelevant as well, although that may not be the case.

Remember, online people make judgments about the website product or service in a matter of seconds. So we must give them what they are looking for quickly.

Not only should the content and design be freshened, but also look at any dates you may have on your pages, such as at the top of the sales letter, many times we use a date in the opening of the letter, or in the copyright of the website.

Both of these areas of the website can easily be automated to dynamically change that information, either using an automated php or JavaScript code block.

This is pretty simple to find via an online search. We recommend the php instance of this code simply because it takes less code and is easier to implement and since it takes less code there is not as much unneeded text for the search engines to go through when spidering.

Biggest Website MISTAKE #21

Not Very Beneficial

This mistake is directed at the sales page but could apply to an entire website.

So many times we miss the boat with this one—we craft a nice looking page and have fairly decent sales copy on the page. But, for whatever reason, we don't seem to be getting the sales we think we should.

Why is that?

Well, one good reason is that the visitor doesn't understand how your product or service benefits them. Too many times we overlook this essential factor when creating our sales letter or sales process. We usually explain what they get and all of the details, but overlook how the consumer can utilize your product or what it does for them.

One thing to think about when writing your benefits is "What problem does your product solve for the buyer?" For example, if you were selling a jacket, you would first have to determine what this jacket does.

Does it provide warmth, style, protection from the rain? Two Pockets; Four Pockets; Zipper or Button? By thinking of those types of things for your product you can easily write a list of benefits to better sell the product.

Just remember to be descriptive of how it helps the buyer, such as by wearing this jacket you will be stylish and warm if you're caught outside on a cool rainy day. We're not professional copywriters, but are sure you get our drift. So many websites miss this element.

When looking at your site as a whole you need to consider "Does the website benefit me or the visitor?" Many times, we create the website based on what is good for us and not necessarily what is good for the visitor.

For example, does the ethical bribe we have for opting in provide a benefit for the person that opts in—or was it just something that we could put up there quickly to complete the site?

By making the site beneficial for the visitor you will increase your conversion as well as improve sales.

Biggest Website MISTAKE #22

Upsell Utopia or Upsell Hell?

This has to be one of the most overlooked mistakes. And it's not the fact that upsells are done wrong. The biggest mistake is that they're not done at all.

First, let's clarify what an "upsell" actually is. An upsell is an offer made at the time of ordering to make additional sales to that visitor.

Think of it like this... If you've ever gone to a fast food restaurant such as McDonalds and you place your order for a hamburger and a drink they always ask "Do you want fries with that?"

That's the best example of an upsell. Think about it—even if you order their combo meal they ask "Would you like an apple pie with that?"

You should have a predetermined upsell item to offer for any of the key items you sell. By doing this, you're making a suggestion of something that would normally go along with that item that is a no-brainer for them to add without thinking. So they add it.

Of course, by applying this strategy you can increase your sales time after time. In many cases sales have increased dramatically. In one case we offered an upsell and 75% of the buyers took it.

We were selling a $97 product and upselling a bundled package for a total of $147 which is, of course, an increase of $50 per sale.

Just imagine if only 25% of 100 buyers took the upsell? Instead of making $9,700 you would make an additional $2,425 simply by suggesting a related item to go along with what they are already buying. The key thing is to make it a related item. You obviously would not offer them steak sauce if they were ordering a fish sandwich.

Another mistake is offering too many items. I've seen several websites where you go from one upsell page to another upsell to yet another upsell. Some call this "Upsell Hell". This strategy causes major confusion.

Just imagine you go to place the order and you are presented with a page with the upsell with two buttons, "Yes take the offer" or "No, I just want the one item" and then you go to another page with another offer and so on.

After some point you either get to place your order, get confused about what you are ordering, or just get frustrated and leave. Obviously this is not a good thing to have happen on your order page.

So be sure to increase your order totals by adding the upsell strategy to your sales process. Just be sure you follow the guidelines above.

You Call This Support?

In our opinion this is beyond a mistake- it's simply a nightmare if you're not providing support or customer service of some sort for the products and/or services you're selling online.

Customer Service doesn't have to be a nightmare. Nor does it have to be time consuming. There are many ways to handle this issue, as well as put a few simple things into place that can limit the number of customer service issues you even need to deal with.

Obviously, the easiest way to handle this would be to outsource your customer support department. A good resource for that would be Workaholics4Hire.com.

But, if you're not quite ready for that level of support and are handling these issues yourself, there are many strategies you can do to head support issues off at the pass.

The first mistake that many website owners make is not having F.A.Q's (Frequently Asked Questions) on their website. This will help eliminate preorder support issues. You can easily generate these questions either from the support issues you've already answered or by running an exit survey on your website.

Another mistake is that the buyer doesn't know how to use the product. You've sold them what they wanted then left them high and dry on how to use it.

You can correct this by creating a simple autoresponder series that explains how to use or consume the product. You can also create an easy member's area that either has step-by-step tutorials or videos that show them how to use the product.

Yet another mistake is not having a ticket system or knowledge base in place. There are several applications that make this really easy.

By having email ticket system all of your responses are received and sent into one central location. This makes it very expandable when you are ready to grow to the next level.

By having a ticket system you can create "canned" responses to questions that come in repeatedly (and they will!). Which, of course, leads to the knowledge base.

This is a data driven system that is included with many of the ticket systems where you can enter the response to the most common questions. The end user can then quickly search through these and never have to submit a ticket in the first place.

Some of the ticket systems that include a knowledge base will automatically watch what the person is typing into the ticket. As they're writing it will try to determine if there's a knowledge base answer for it and display it just above the submit button.

This also greatly reduces the number of support tickets you receive. One of the ticket systems we recommend is kayako.com.

Section #5

A Touch of Technical Stuff

- Headline HTML

- Image alt tags Missing in Action

- Not Compressing Images

- Missing or Poor Use of Your Web Page Title

- Getting in "Jive" with Javascript

- Poor or No SEO

Biggest Website MISTAKE #24

Headline HTML

When laying out a web page many marketers neglect to use the right html tags with their headlines and subheads. Yeah, that may sound scary and technical, but it really isn't and it can make a big difference in your search engine rankings.

Many times people set their entire page as normal paragraphs and don't designate the headlines differently. Here's what we mean....

If you look at the code view of many web pages you would see something like this....

<p>"Learn the Hidden Secrets to Writing

Award Winning Headlines by Using the Same

Strategies Top Internet Marketers Use!"</p>

<p> Hi welcome to my website I want to tell you about my product blah blah blah you get the point</p>

<p>"Here's Why a Headline Swipe File is a No Brainer"</p>

<p>More text explaining why you want to start a headline swipe file, blah blah blah</p>

What you see above is the simple html code for part of a sales page. The "<p>" tag is HTML to tell the browser that the following text is a paragraph and the "</p>" tell the browser that it is the end of that paragraph.

This is all well and good but nothing about it tells the browser where the headlines or sub headlines are. Believe it or not, the search engines look for that.

Here is a good example of how the above HTML should look.

<h1>"Learn the Hidden Secrets to Writing

Award Winning Headlines by Using the Same

Strategies Top Internet Marketers Use!"</h1>

<p>Hi welcome to my website I want to tell you about my product blah blah blah you get the point</p>

<h2>"Here's Why a Headline Swipe File is A No Brainer"</h2>

<p>More text explaining why you want to start a headline swipe file, blah blah blah</p>

You can see that "<h1>" and "<h2>" tags have been added to designate where the headline and sub headlines are. You can use additional "h" tags but that is another discussion.

By adding the appropriate "h" tags the search engines can quickly determine the importance of that text over the regular paragraph text and it will make a big difference in your search engine ranking.

Obviously, you will only want to use the <h1> tag for the headline and the <h2> tag for each sub headline afterwards.

Biggest Website MISTAKE #25

Image alt Tags Missing in Action

Let's start this section by describing what an image alternate (alt) tag is before going into its purpose.

When the Internet was in its early stages everything on the web was text because connection speeds were limited. As technology improved so did web pages. At that point more and more sites began to use images on their web pages. Unfortunately, many users still had slow dial up connections.

Since some web visitors had these slower connections they would turn off the ability for images to load in their web browser so that web pages would load more quickly. That's where the alternative tags (alt tags) come into play.

A website owner would add a tag to their web page code for the image to display some descriptive text as an alternative to the image itself, so that if the images were turned off the web page still made sense to the reader.

Today, some website owners still add alt text to their pages, but for a different reason. The alt text is more of a complement to the image rather than an alternative.

With today's technology, when you hover your mouse over an object without clicking the alt text will be displayed as a small text box floating over the image in most browsers.

Most people just add an image descriptor. There isn't anything wrong with doing this, but what many people forget to do for its marketing value is add keywords to the alt tag.

Why is this important? Keywords are buzzwords that visitors use in search engines to find your site. What many website owners don't realize is that the search engines read your alt tags too.

So, the alt tag is forgotten real estate many marketers forget about that could attract additional visitors to their site.

It doesn't take an experienced web programmer to add an alt tag to your web page images.

Here's an example of HTML code for a normal image WITHOUT an alt tag.

Now here's a sample of HTML code WITH an alt tag inserted.

```
<img src="http://www.that1domain.com/sampleimage.gif"
alt="This image shows web resources you need">
```

Not much difference between the two. But by adding the alt tag you add another mention of one of your keyword phrases (in this example, "web resources") to your page, therefore improving your chances of higher search engine rankings.

Not Compressing Images

One of the biggest mistakes website owners make is putting images on their website that have not been compressed for web usage. You may have visited a website where the image seems to take forever to fill in or appears to paint in as the image loads. This is because the image wasn't properly formatted for the website. Any image that you are going to use on a website should be saved at 72 dpi (dpi = dots per inch).

There are many applications that you can get that will allow you to "Save for Web", which reduces an image to the 72 dpi setting.

Something else to consider is the actual size of the image. Almost everyone these days has a digital camera, so we have photos readily available. One thing we generally don't consider is the actual size of these images.

Here's an example. If you have a 7 megapixel camera and leave it at the default setting most likely that camera will take a picture that is 3072 pixels by 2304 pixels. Now compare that to your most common computer screen setting, which is currently 1024 pixels by 768 pixels.

You can see there is a huge difference in visual size. Now take into account also that the original image is 1.8 Megabytes (MB) in size. Depending on the connection speed that image could take up to 4 minutes and 29 seconds to download if your visitor is on a dial-up connection and 39 seconds to download if your visitor has DSL.

Simply by "Saving for Web" allows you to reduce the file size to 594 Kilobytes (KB), which will reduce the download time to 1 minute 26 seconds on dial-up and 12 seconds on DSL. But the image would still be 3 times larger than your web browser. What some website owners do is use HTML to make the image appear to fit on the page.

Even using a WYSIWYG (What You See Is What You Get) editor like Microsoft's FrontPage (now called Web Expressions) or Adobe's Dreamweaver you can "tell" the page to make the image a set size to fit the page even though the image is still the original size.

To get the best image that downloads fast and looks good use a photo editing application to resize the image. For instance, if you design a web page that is 800 pixels wide you can easily put an image on the page that is 450 pixels wide and still have room for text around the image.

By resizing the image to 450 pixels wide AND saving for the web you can reduce that image down to 40 KB, which even on dial-up will take only 5 seconds to download.

Biggest Website MISTAKE #27

Missing or Poor Use of Your Web Page Title

This may well be the biggest mistake we see. Or, at least, it's the one that bugs us the most.

This mistake is happening right now literally over 500 million times on the Internet. That's right – 500 million.

What is this mistake? It's poor use of or not using your web page title.

The web page title is what is displayed in the upper left corner of your web browser application.

For example, if you are using Internet Explorer or Firefox and visit the website 50BiggestMistakes.com you will see at the very top of your browser window the icon for the browser application and the words "50 Biggest Mistakes | Information Marketing Mistakes – Internet Explorer (or Mozilla Firefox).

This may seem trivial to you but the fact is that the title of your website is the first thing most search engines look at or spider when they come to your web page.

Earlier we mentioned this is happening right now over 500 million times on the web. Want proof?

Do this little experiment. Open up your favorite web browser. Go to Google.com or Yahoo.com and in the search box enter the phrase "untitled document" and click the search button.

At the time this was being written the results came back with 30,500,000 listings. Untitled document is the default page name for Adobe Dreamweaver's web page application.

Microsoft FrontPage uses "New Page" so you might imagine you would find a lot of results for that as well. No need to imagine. The current search turns up 15,000,000 listings for "new page" right now.

Simply by not entering a web page title when your site was first created reduces your chances of the search engines finding and ranking your site high on their list.

An even bigger mistake than a missing web page title made by Internet marketers is poorly using your web page title.

Here's another little experiment for you. In your browser's search box type in the phrase "Welcome to". At the time of this writing this phrase returned 530,000,000 results. Now there is nothing wrong with welcoming people to your website, but if you're trying to get found, why would you want this to be part of your web page title? Wouldn't you want to make sure you use every possible advantage you can?

So how do you fix this?

If you're doing this yourself (vs. having your webmaster fix it), we recommend downloading your web page from your website to make sure you have the current version. If you're unsure about doing this hire a webmaster, read up on using FTP software, or visit <u>www.EasyWebCourse.com</u>.

If you're ready to tackle this yourself open up the page in your favorite web page editing software. (Or you can do this in notepad as well).

At the top of the page in code view you will see <title>Untitled Document</title> (or something like this). Replace what is there with the desired title, preferably something that is keyword rich for your product or niche, and then upload that page to your website. Be sure to check it in your web browser to be sure it displays properly. Finally, test to see what works best.

Biggest Website MISTAKE #28

Getting in "Jive" with JavaScript

This website mistake is more on the geeky side so bear with us. It's important to cover because it will help the effectiveness of your web page. Not so much for the website visitor, but to the search engine spiders and how easily your web page code is spidered.

When a search engine visits your page it's looking to find out anything about your page or website it possibly can to determine if it has usable content and if the information is relevant to the keywords you have listed.

To understand this you need to have a basic understanding of JavaScript. **JavaScript** is a programming language used for client-side web development. JavaScript is a trademark of Sun Microsystems. It was used under license for technology invented and implemented by Netscape Communications and current entities such as the Mozilla Foundation.

Microsoft has its own version called Jscript. JavaScript is useful to automate certain elements on a web page and to add some web "magic" to your site. An example is having the date on your sales letter page always showing today's date. Or, a pop up window that opens up when you click a link.

JavaScript can be quite lengthy when putting the code in place to make something happen on the web page dynamically. Imagine the search engine having to wade through hundreds, if not thousands, of extra lines of JavaScript code to figure out what your web page is really saying.

This doesn't have to happen and in most cases shouldn't happen. We're not saying not to use JavaScript, but are saying it's important to use what is called an "include" for your JavaScript.

This allows you to take the JavaScript and put it on its own page or actually a file and "include" it using a statement on your web page. The web browser reads this method exactly as the other method but it provides much cleaner "code" for you to work with and allows the search engines to see more of what you really want them to spider.

You can easily achieve this by copying the JavaScript code seen in the HTML version of your page and pasting it into a notepad or WordPad application and then saving the page as a .js file such as yourcode.js.

Then, in the same location you removed the code from, you would add a statement to the page like this:

```
<script type="text/javascript" src="yourcode.js"> </script>
```

It's important to make sure to have the "type" listed to make it valid code, but it is most important that you have the "src" (source) path correct. Otherwise, the JavaScript will not be found and will not work at all.

Biggest Website MISTAKE #29

Poor or No SEO

This is a common mistake, simply due to the fact that many website owners are unaware of what SEO actually is and how it applies to them or their site.

First off, let's clarify that SEO is actually an abbreviation for *Search Engine Optimization* and means optimizing one's website or web pages so that it can easily be indexed organically in the search engines.

There are certain techniques or strategies you can apply to your web pages that will increase the amount of traffic you receive from the search engines. Let's go ahead and cover some of the basic areas where SEO techniques are commonly overlooked.

The Title tag is one of the most important, as well as one of the most overlooked. Be sure to have your main keyword as close to the first part of your title as possible.

Another key area that is often overlooked is the Meta tags section. This is a section that contains the description of the website, as well as the keywords for your site. This area is not seen by the website visitor. It's a section found at the upper part of the HTML code section for your web pages.

"H" tags are often forgotten. Many search engines look for "H1" and "H2" tags when reviewing your site to see what relevant content you may have headlines for. (That's what the "H" stands for on those tags "Headline")

There are many SEO elements that can be applied but let's cover just a couple more. One spot where you can add information to increase keyword relevancy is the alt tag on each of your images. If you are unfamiliar with alt tags be sure to check out the section on Images and Alt tags.

Finally, a good way to improve search engine traffic is to have a sitemap for your site. A sitemap is simply a page containing links to all of the pages on your site with the appropriate title as the link name.

There is a lot that could be said about improving SEO on your website and a simple search on Google for "organic search engine optimization tips" will give you plenty of information on this topic.

Other Image Issues

- What Type of Image Do You Want?

- Linking Images

- Outdated/Unflattering Photos

Biggest Website MISTAKE #30

What Type of Image Do You Want?

Web image types—JPG vs. GIF vs. PNG

There are three types of image formats that are widely used for web graphics. These are; jpg or jpeg; gif and png (pronounced as ping). We'll explain each in just a moment along with their uses.

We're sure you've visited a website where a person's picture looked pixelated or spotted. Or an image had ragged edges, or even yet an image on a colored background that had a white border to it.

The reason is that the right image type was not used for the right purposes. Below you will discover the right reasons to use each of the web approved file formats.

JPEG/JPG Images

JPG files are best for photos. If you're using a photo that has a lot of detail, say of a person or of scenery, JPGs will give you the best picture quality for the image size. JPG files are formatted to allow more color combinations than the other formats, so that's why you'll see a greater difference in image quality.

Short for *Joint Photographic Experts Group*, the original name of the committee that wrote the standard. JPG is one of the image file formats supported on the Web. JPG is a lossy compression technique that is designed to compress color and grayscale continuous-tone images. The information that is discarded in the compression is information that the human eye cannot detect.

JPG images support 16 million colors and are best suited for photographs and complex graphics. The user typically has to compromise on either the quality of the image or the size of the file. JPG does not work well on line drawings, lettering or simple graphics because there is not a lot of the image that can be thrown out in the lossy process, so the image loses clarity and sharpness.

GIF Images

GIF files are best suited for images that have more text than detail or for simple graphics like iconic style clip art. Since the GIF file format allows for less color combinations, images with a lot of gradient color will seem not as sharp and may appear to have bands or lines, when a color goes from lighter to darker over a short span.

GIF images are best known on the web for their animation ability. Any of the animated banners you see on the Internet are either GIF files or flash. Flash is actually an animated movie and the file size is generally greater than that of a flash file.

Flash files also require a special player to be viewed which is why most designers stick with the GIF format for simple banner animation.

GIF is short for *Graphics Interchange Format*, another of the graphics formats supported by the Web. Unlike JPG, the GIF format is a lossless compression technique and it supports only 256 colors.

GIF is better than JPG for images with only a few distinct colors, such as line drawings, black and white images and small text that are only a few pixels high.

With an animation editor, GIF images can be put together for animated images. GIF also supports *transparency*, where the background color can be set to transparent in order to let the color on the underlying Web page show through.

The compression algorithm used in the GIF format is owned by Unisys, and companies that use the algorithm are supposed to license the use from Unisys.

PNG Images

PNG graphics are best known for their file size quality and transparency capabilities and are now being supported by all of the newest browser versions. More designers seem to be using PNGs more frequently but in comparison to using PNG over JPG for images the PNG file size for the quality is still larger.

Overall, the PNG file format is a faster alternative for standard web images.

PNG is short for *Portable Network Graphics*, the third graphics standard supported by the Web. PNG was developed as a patent-free answer to the GIF format but is also an improvement on the GIF technique.

An image in a lossless PNG file can be 5%-25% more compressed than a GIF file of the same image.

PNG builds on the idea of transparency in GIF images and allows the control of the degree of transparency, known as *opacity*. Saving, restoring and resaving a PNG image will not degrade its quality. PNG does not support animation like GIF does.

Biggest Website
MISTAKE #31

Linking Images

Have you ever visited a website and seen a place where an image should be but you see a big red X instead or an icon with a broken link or something like that?

Well, in some cases it is something as simple as the file wasn't uploaded or uploaded to the wrong location, or is being hosted on a third party site and that site is inaccessible at the time.

But, in many cases, it's just a problem with a bad link structure. In some web page software the image gets linked to the web page designer's hard drive and not the path to the image on the server.

This, of course, will cause a problem when the page is uploaded, BUT to the designer the page will look fine because the browser on his computer will be able to find the image because it's pointing to a location on his or her own hard drive.

In most cases this happens because the image is added to the page before the web page is saved. We've seen this in testing many web design applications.

So a good rule of thumb to keep this from happening is when working with a new page from scratch, be sure to save the page after you open it. That "should" keep this from happening.

Let's talk about what an incorrect link looks like and then what the correct link should be. Obviously, the incorrect link will vary as will the correct link, but if you understand what you're looking for that will help correct this issue or keep it from happening in the first place.

In most cases the incorrect link will look similar to this <img src="c:\my documents\pictures\picturename.jpg">.

You may see something with file= in the URL but it will be similar to the above. Two things to notice are that it is pointing to a local drive letter c: or d: or whichever drive letter the image was on. Also notice the direction of the slash "\" if it is local it will use a back slash "\" if it is a web or net work URL it is a forward slash "/".

A correct link will use what is called an absolute or relative URL. Without getting too technical let's explain the two terms and then move forward. An absolute URL is one that is not dependent on any other information. An absolute URL uses the exact location on the website where the image is hosted.

Here's an example. If linking to the logo on my blog (FrankDeardurff.com) you would give the exact path to the image that was uploaded to the images folder. This would be:

> **http://frankdeardurff.com/images/owgdude.png.**

You could put that URL into any browser and without a doubt it would display that image in the browser window. That is an absolute URL.

So if you were looking in your HTML source code the above image would appear as

```
<img src="http://frankdeardurff.com/images/owgdude.png">
```

A relative URL can get a little tricky because you're linking to the image as it is related to the root of the web directory. (Sounds confusing already, huh?)

First, lets look at the relative URL for the same image above. The relative URL would appear as:

```
../images/owgdude.png
```

or if you were to look at the HTML source code:

```
<img src="../images/owgdude.png">
```

The URL is shorter but you will need to be aware of how the image relates to the root folder. The ".." tells the server to go up one level from root to the find the images folder.

Using relative URLs can get a little more confusing if you're using subfolders or sub domains. You just need to be fully aware where the image is located.

Obviously, either method will work as long as you use them correctly. Both methods have their advantages and disadvantages but you can easily see how some images can be incorrectly linked from time to time.

Biggest Website MISTAKE #32

Outdated/Unflattering Photos

Has this happened to you? You go to an event where a known author is scheduled to attend. You bring a copy of his or her book to get signed. The author isn't scheduled to speak until the last day of the event, so you carry the book around with you the whole weekend in hopes of spotting the author.

Here's where the problem begins. You're scouring the crowd in search of the person matching the photo on the back of the book and they're nowhere to be found. So, at this point you're thinking they either don't want to be found or they won't be there until the day they're speaking.

Then comes the day of their presentation and the person they introduce looks NOTHING like the person on the back of the book. It's obvious the picture on the book jacket is from 20 years earlier. Not only is this a total let down, it also creates a disconnect in multiple ways.

The same thing can happen on your website. By using an image from your earlier days where you thought you looked better or younger, you may create the same disconnect.

The potential client will feel cheated or lied to when they finally meet you in person and they realize the person they thought they knew wasn't really that person.

Although it's hard for some of us to accept, we do get older. We may be 20 years old in our head but our appearance does change. We just have to deal with it!

One key thing to remember people buy from those they know, like and TRUST. Don't blow it by using an image that is no longer you.

Here are some things to consider that will improve your photographic appearance. Don't use a snapshot for your website. Good lighting will help, as will dressing in business attire that matches your business model.

That means you need to look the part you're portraying. Don't overdress but don't wear a t-shirt in your promotional pictures either.

You don't need to spend a lot of money either to create a good photo image for your website. I'm sure there is a local department store in your area that has a basic package that will work for what you need.

Even better, if you attend any of the major marketing events, check in advance to see if Visible Impact Photography will be there. Mary Mazzullo is the founder of that company and knows the correct poses you see on the top marketers' websites.

That way you can grow your business by networking at the event and grow your web image by getting the correct photos that show who you really are and that will make a lasting impression.

Some Troubles with Testimonials

- Leading People Away from Your Site with Your Testimonials
- Plain Jane Testimonials

Biggest Website MISTAKE #33

Leading People Away from Your Site with Your Testimonials

Now here's a mistake you need to look at from two different sides. This one has to do with testimonials. If you're giving a testimonial to someone else what you hope for is completely opposite of what you want to do when someone gives you a testimonial for use on your site.

As a giver of a testimonial you hope that the other website owner will link to your website through your testimonial. Of course, in your testimonial itself you want to say something like "Hi, this is Frank Deardurff, co-founder of AskDatabase.com and I'd like to tell you about…"

At the end of your printed testimonial on their site you're going to have your name and website URL. You hope that the URL is a live link directly to your website. They shouldn't, but you hope that they do.

However, on your site you don't EVER want to have a live link in the testimonials about your product. Why would you want to provide your visitor with another easily clickable distraction that takes them away from your sales letter? You don't, so any URL you have listed with a testimonial on your site should NEVER be a live link. ANY type of external links you have within your site runs the risk of leading a visitor away, never to return.

Biggest Website MISTAKE #34

Plain Jane Testimonials

Credibility of the testimonials on your sales page is critical to your entire sales process. So many websites have just a basic text testimonial that could be written by anybody. It doesn't matter if you've included their first and last name, city and business. It just doesn't look credible.

The most basic of text testimonials will have something like Jane N. as the name of the person providing the testimonial. These have zero credibility. Even if you've added a city and state to it like "Jane N., Boulder, CO" it doesn't climb very far up the credibility ladder.

It's so important to add a picture of the person providing the testimonial and, if at all possible, an audio. The audio can be exactly what their written testimonial says in spoken format. It's next to impossible to manufacture a testimonial that has an audio with it. Therefore, more credible.

And, with video becoming even more popular, video testimonials will have even higher credibility and probably improve conversion on any sales page. But, as we discussed before, be sure to TEST it.

Don't overlook the importance of testimonials on your website. A second rate effort on your testimonials will lead to second rate results in your sales.

Getting Maximum Value from Your Website

- Wasted Opt-out Pages

- Not Using Your Website as a Continual Testing Ground

- Video Mistakes

- Thankless Thank You Pages

- Build It and They Will Come. Or Will They?

- Oops on Your Opt-in Page

- Lost Pages / 404 Error Pages

- Not Asking

Wasted Opt-out Pages

Okay, we're as guilty as the next person of this mistake, but after recently deleting 6,000 eMails from an inbox that had accumulated over a five month period without being read and opting out of several newsletters that weren't read anymore due to being too busy or lost interest we noticed a huge website mistake that probably 95% of all marketers are making.

What is this mistake?

Simply, we don't take advantage of our opt-out pages or the opt-out confirmation pages.

We leave them blank or use the autoresponder service's ugly default page. Why not try a few things on this page to keep that valuable name in your marketing funnel?

Here are a few suggestions:

- On the page they visit to opt-out remind them of the value of what they originally opted-in for. Maybe they've simply forgotten and in a bit of a rush just decided to opt-out.

- Try using audio on this page or something else that grabs their attention. If the original opt-in was for a free report, audio, or something they downloaded give them a link to it again right here. You've got nothing to lose.

- Put an ASK campaign (See AskDatabase.com) here asking them why they are deciding to opt out. Let them know that after filling in their question you'll provide the link to opt out on the thank you page.

- If they decide to opt-out without giving you feedback put a different offer to one of your products or an affiliate offer on the opt-out confirmation page. Maybe they'll check it out. If they do give you feedback put the offer on that page as well. Maybe what they originally opted in for wasn't what they were wanting but the new offer might be.

Give them something to click on other than the opt-out link. Obviously, the opt-out link needs to be there also, but we've seen too many pages that just show a simple blank page with nothing on it but the opt-out link.

And, the confirmation page is just as sparse with nothing for them to do but close the window. Why not open that window to opportunity!

Biggest Website MISTAKE #36

Not Using Your Website as a Continual Testing Ground

Testing is an often overlooked or completely forgotten about function of a website. You should always be in "test mode" on your website, tweaking and testing to see what you can do to improve conversion rates.

Any element of your web page can and should be tested to see if you can get a better response from your website visitors.

An example is your website background. Test it to see if your opt-ins or sales improve or decrease when switching from the current background color (let's say white) to a grey background.

If the grey gets better conversion then test grey against blue, grey versus green, and so on until you find the optimal color for the best conversion for your market.

Next try modifying your headline. Test header graphic versus no header graphic. Obviously, there are a lot of things to test and different variations of testing will eventually reward you with the best sales conversion possible.

Of course, it's most important to get something up on your web page. Then, and only then, do you start testing, tweaking and improving. Obviously, it is best to have some traffic coming to the site so you have something to base your tests from.

There are different ways to test, whether it is to have a group of close friends or a mastermind group review the page. Most of your web hosting packages have statistical applications. If they don't either ask them or look for hosting that does.

You would find these stats packages in the control panel for your website. If you need web hosting we recommend Hostorix. com, as they have everything that an online business owner would need. You can also use free applications like Google Analytics. You'll be pleasantly surprised at the information you can find when reviewing the data gathered from your web stats.

There is additional software that you can use to track every single link on your website and even use what are called "heat maps" on your website to track mouse movement on the website to see the "hot spots" on your webpage from your visitor traffic.

The key mistake here we're trying to emphasize is that of not doing any tracking or testing at all on your site. You should ALWAYS be in test mode in some way.

Biggest Website MISTAKE #37

Video Mistakes

With more people using video on their websites here's a mistake we see over and over again.

First, let's be clear we think using video on your website is a good idea, as long as it's done correctly. Many times we see video that has been put on the page below the fold of the website. (Hidden below the bottom edge of the screen).

This is okay, but not when the video is set to automatically play!

The BIGGEST mistake we see people make with putting video on their websites is they are using a service like YouTube™, which is okay in itself, but they put the video code on the page as is. What happens when you do this is that when the video finishes it shows related videos the visitor can click on.

This is bad for multiple reasons. Most importantly is the fact that the user now has a choice to watch a related video or continue through your sales process... hmm what choice do you think is made here?

The second issue is that the related video shown could very well be your competitor's video selling a similar product! Now your visitor has yet another option, not only to watch another video but possibly get interested in someone else's product.

Okay, before you go out and rip down all your YouTube™ type videos from your web pages read on because there is an easy correction. When getting the "embed" code for your video click the small gear icon next to that URL. That is the "customize" button. This will allow you to check the check box that says "Include related videos", you can select some other options there as well like whether to show a border or to pick a different size to play.

Once you have these settings the way you want them, grab the URL and post that on your page. And, of course, upload the new page to your site and watch the video all the way through to make sure you see the expected results.

Finally, don't assume your web visitor knows how video players work. You want to make it simple so any level of web visitor can see the video. You can do this by adding a line of text (in a smaller font) that says "click the play button with the triangle to watch this video". We'd even suggest adding an icon of the button or an arrow pointing to the button.

We know this seems simple, but the visual command will actually get you more plays of the video.

Biggest Website
MISTAKE #38

Thankless Thank You Pages

Another mistake we see time after time is either no thank you page or a thank you page with not much on it. In the past, we've purchased an online or digital product and after the purchase we were redirected either back to the website or to a page that simply said "Check your email for details about your purchase".

In the first case, if you're redirected back to the home page or elsewhere you're wondering if your order went through and, if so, when will you get your download? The second question is WHEN will you get the email? Who will it be from and what should you look for?

Why would you want to leave your new customer guessing?

Here are a few things to consider when creating your thank you page, whether it be for an optin, purchase or product download.

First, congratulate them on their success. For example "Thanks for registering" or "Thank you for your purchase". If you have the ability to personalize it with their name, such as "Thanks for Registering Joe!" then do so.

Then acknowledge what just happened, i.e. "You've just opted in for our Marketing Newsletter" followed by what to expect. "Soon you'll be receiving an email with the details of your purchase... it will be from email@that1domain.com. You should white list this address. If you need instructions click here".

Ideally, if they have just made a purchase from you it's best to automate this process. You could have a member name and password generated which is provided with a login link on the thank you page for them to access a member's area to pick up their purchase. That method requires putting some other systems in place.

Finally, if you are giving them instructions via email, then give them something else to click on from this page. For example, if they've just opted in to an email list tell them they can get more information by visiting your blog, to which of course you'd want to add a link.

If they have just made a purchase maybe suggest another product or services of yours you think would work well with what they just purchased.

In any case, give them something to do when they get to this page. Give them the necessary information to confirm and reassure them they are getting what they took action on.

By doing this you will have less customer support issues and create a greater relationship with your customer right from the start.

Biggest Website MISTAKE #39

Build It and They Will Come. Or Will They?

That saying is not only a quote from the movie "Field of Dreams", but also the thought process for many website owners. And, unfortunately, website owners are "dreaming" if they think this is true.

Many times web business owners feel they have a great product, service or information and build a great website and wonder why they don't have visitors. Well, the fact is, just because you know about it doesn't mean the search engines know about it. And, of course, if the search engines don't know about your website, neither will your potential customers.

Of course, the old saying for offline businesses is true about online businesses, and that is it's all about location, location, location!

Offline businesses buy or rent space at prime locations to have a fair amount of people drive by their store with a chance they'll stop in and make a purchase. This is the same strategy we use online as well, except the space that we rent or buy is located in the search engines. We're talking about buying Google AdWords,

Banner ads, Ezine Ads and other digital locations where we can purchase ad space.

By putting yourself in front of the traffic your clients can't help but "drive" by and check out your "offerings" for sale or consumption.

Buying traffic is just one way to get visitors to your website. There is the old fashioned way of submitting your website to the search engines. Many of the search engines such as Google still have the web submit form to have your site reviewed by that search engine.

One such place is:

> **http://www.google.com/addurl**

That will get Google to come out and "spider" or search your site for relevant keywords. Another way to improve traffic is via search engine optimization, as well as article submission, blog posts and comment posting.

By applying these simple techniques you will have plenty of traffic coming to your site in no time at all.

Biggest Website MISTAKE #40

Oops on Your Opt-in Page

Okay, so not everyone uses opt-in pages for their websites (which, in our opinion, is a mistake in itself) so we'll explain quickly what they are.

These are the pages that you would put as the main page of your website. Some people call these landing pages, name capture pages, or even squeeze pages.

Marketers and business owners use these pages to reveal details of the product or service and offer the visitor a free chapter, report, white paper, audio, video or something such as that.

To get this freebie offer the visitor must "opt-in" by putting their name and email address in a form on that page and submitting the form. That is, in short terms, what an "opt-in" page is.

So the biggest mistake with opt-in pages would be not using them. By utilizing an opt-in page you can quickly and easily start building a relationship with that potential client. This also helps get rid of "tire kickers" as they're called.

These are people that are a little bit interested, but not interested enough to take the next step to opt-in. Case studies show that if they won't even give you their email address then there's an even slimmer chance they would part with their money.

Another mistake on opt-in pages is not giving an ethical bribe of value, or saying enough about what that report or audio freebie you're giving away entails. You need to look at the opt-in page as a mini sales letter for the giveaway.

This leads to yet another common mistake with opt-ins and that is the "Free Report" that has nothing to do with the product or service you want them to actually buy from you in the end. Ideally, the report should promote and lead them back to the sales page to purchase. Think of it as an info brochure someone would pick up in store to get more details.

Of course, this goes hand in hand with not having an auto responder sequence tied into the opt-in form to follow up with them about the free report getting them to devour that information and coaxing them back into your sales process.

One of the BIGGEST mistakes we see when using an opt-in page is that the form takes the visitor to a thank you / confirmation page and not the sales letter. This is the quickest way to kill the sale. The visitor wants immediate information so don't make them wait.

There are many more mistakes we can think of on opt-in pages as that could be a training course in itself. But we want to leave you with one more critical opt-in mistake and that would be no audio on the page.

You will want to put a simple audio on the page welcoming them to the site and "quickly" telling them who you are and about whatever it is you're offering them, as well as how to get it.

Step them through filling out the form (yeah, that seems like a no brainer but it works) and then tell them how they will receive what they are signing up for and what to expect on the next page.

This will help you quickly build your list and build a good relationship with a potential client faster than you would imagine possible.

Biggest Website MISTAKE #41

Lost Pages / 404 Errors

"Page Not Found" This is something just about everyone has seen at one time or another if you've spent anytime online at all. The web term for this type of page is a 404-page.

Now you are probably thinking why is a "page not found" or a 404 error page a website mistake, and that would be a fair question to ask. So let us explain what this mistake is, how you can benefit from it, and how to correct it.

First, we've already mentioned "what" it is but let me explain how "people" get there. 404s are usually found either from a broken link on your website somewhere or when someone has tried to type in a URL to a specific page on your site, and has either mistyped it or the page is no longer there.

It is possible that you will see in your stats that there have been requests for your robot.txt fie which is a common file that search engine spiders look for, and if you don't have one then a 404 page would be triggered.

Now to explain how 404 pages can "help" you. There is a lot of discussion about what should or shouldn't be displayed on your 404 page or if you should even display the error page.

Our opinion is to display the page but have key elements on the page, such as a logo or look and feel of your website, along with a message saying that the page they are looking for was not found but click here to go to the home page of your website.

Another option is if the visitor hits your 404 page, automatically redirect them to the home page of your website. This option works really well, but in discussions we've heard people say that the visitor is a little confused as to what just happened.

By utilizing the custom 404 page, you don't miss out on the opportunity to connect with that visitor. Without any information on that page the visitor would just enter something else into the web address bar and go elsewhere.

The easiest way to remedy this issue is to log into your control panel (cpanel) and look for the icon that says "Error Pages". This will list all of them. Be sure to click the 404 and enter your information there. If you are unsure what to put there you can search Google to see some examples.

If you're uncomfortable doing this you can easily hire a programmer from rent-a-coder.com or getafreelancer.com to quickly do this for you. It is a quick project and once you have a template you can copy and paste it into your other sites.

Biggest Website MISTAKE #42

Not Asking!

This mistake happens, not just online, but offline as well. For now we'll focus about the online version of this mistake.

The mistake we're talking about is not "Asking" your customers. Let's clarify a bit more. When a visitor comes to your website and doesn't buy, you have no clue why. Correct? Well if you "Ask" them, in most cases, they will tell you.

Our good friend and mentor Armand Morin launched one of his sites a few years ago (audiogenerator.com). He'd already predetermined what he was going to sell the product for, which was $29.95, but when he launched the site he wasn't getting the sales he thought he would.

So, to find out why people were leaving without buying he put in place what's called an exit survey.

What this does is this—if a website visitor leaves the page without clicking the order button a small window is launched. This small window has one simple question, "Wait, before you go what's the single biggest reason you are leaving without giving Audio Generator a fair try?".

By asking this one question Armand was able to determine the challenge the visitors were having, and instead of lowering the price, made one small change in the headline copy that increased sales dramatically.

Of course, there are many other reasons to "Ask" your prospects and customers to get valuable information that you can use to give them what they want. Here are a few quick examples.

Creating a Product? Don't assume you know what information your niche market wants—ask them. For example, you could ask: "What's the single biggest question you have about starting an online business?" Obviously you would modify that for your niche.

Hosting a Teleseminar? Again, a similar question—"What's your greatest challenge with meeting your deadlines?" Take the top 10 -12 questions and answer them on a call. You already know the answers because it's a topic in your niche and now you're providing the content your market asked for!

These are just a couple examples of how you can simply "Ask" your customers what they're thinking and then deliver it to them. Or, adjust your processes accordingly to increase the results you BOTH are looking for.

The best way we have found to "Ask" your customers is a service called AskDatabase.com. They have a 21-day trial you can check out for just $1!

Section #9

Some "Gotta Have It" Factors

- No Contact Information
- I Guarantee It
- Legally Speaking

Biggest Website MISTAKE #43

No Contact Information

This is a pretty simple mistake that you see not just on websites, but in autoresponder emails as well. Just to clarify – We're talking about not having your contact information available for the reader to see.

Many website owners are skeptical about putting contact information on their website because they're concerned with getting their email address spammed from automated "bots" that surf the web harvesting those addresses.

There are ways to handle that—such as email encryption scripts that will take your email address and make it hidden or scrambled to such robot harvesters. Another option is to just create a contact form on your site that you link to from the footer of your website. That way you don't have to display your email address and the visitor can still reach you.

In some cases we've even seen where the website owner will have their contact link go to their support desk which may be the best solution because then all responses are in a centralized location, so that either you or your support team can answer them promptly.

We mentioned adding your contact information in your auto responder messages and or email newsletters. This is a requirement now with the Can-Spam Act. That is a funny title for rules and guidelines for cutting out spam. But it actually stands for Controlling the Assault of Non-Solicited Pornography and Marketing Act.

It states in the Can-Spam act:

"**It requires that commercial email be identified as an advertisement and include the sender's valid physical postal address.** Your message must contain clear and conspicuous notice that the message is an advertisement or solicitation and that the recipient can opt out of receiving more commercial email from you. It also must include your valid physical postal address."

We haven't seen as many emails stating that it's an advertisement but have seen more and more online business making sure to add their physical address to their mailings and website.

Of course, the main reason you'll want to add contact information is that some buyers just have questions before purchasing. Or, maybe something is broken on your site and they can't order. It's a good idea if you get many questions asked over and over to include a "Frequently Ask Questions" (FAQ) section in your website. This will convert the sale quicker and cut down on support requests.

Biggest Website
MISTAKE #44

I Guarantee It

A common mistake on many websites is that of either a non-existent or weak guarantee.

There are many misconceptions about using a guarantee on a website. We've heard some discussion about the fact that if they add a guarantee to their website they are afraid that brings to light the possibility that the buyer can return the product.

We think that's the furthest thing from the truth. In fact, by not having a guarantee on your website you make the buyer think that the product is a possible scam OR you do not have enough faith in the product to warrant a guarantee.

Of course, there is always the possibility you simply forgot to add the guarantee to your website. Here are some things to consider when creating or updating the guarantee you have.

Most merchant accounts and payment processors want or require you to have a guarantee policy easily displayed on your website. Be sure to check out what they require and adjust accordingly.

Be sure to make your guarantee "look" like a guarantee policy. Many times we see this section look like the normal sales copy on the page. Or, if there is a box around it, it resembles the other boxes on the page.

What we've found to work well is add an image that resembles a certificate as a background image or create (or have created) the whole thing as a graphic to easily place all of the elements you want in that area.

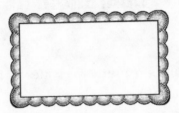

Also what is appealing is to add an official seal to that area. You can easily find these at either istockphoto.com or fotolia.com. Both of these stock photo websites will allow you to purchase at a very reasonable price both the certificate and seal images to use on your website.

Finally, don't leave any doubt about what your policy is, explain the details and be sure that it fits the offer. You wouldn't use the same policy for a live event, teleseminar or webinar that you would for say an ebook, physical product, or services rendered.

Simply do a little research into what others are doing and then modify to meet your needs and, of course, test to see what gets you the best conversions.

Biggest Website
MISTAKE #45

Legally Speaking

This mistake is pretty common across most websites on the web today. We know we've gotten in a hurry ourselves and made this mistake, but it's critical to be sure not to make this mistake and it is easily remedied.

What we're talking about here is the required legal mumbo jumbo on our websites.

Not only is it a good suggestion but in many cases it is required by your merchant account and, in the United States, the Federal Trade Commission.

Let's get a little more specific about what we're talking about. You should make it a common practice to add the correct notifications about your Privacy Policy, Earnings Disclaimer and Terms of Service. It's also a good idea to add your business contact information.

The Privacy Policy helps build trust with your website visitors and shows that you are professional and trustworthy. This policy should state things about what information you collect, how the information is used or not used, how you protect the info you do collect and things such as that.

The Earnings Disclaimer should spell out in detail that you do not guarantee that your product or service will give them a set level of income and that you accurately state what is possible or if income is possible.

Terms of Service simply states what your acceptable use policies are for your products and how they are handled, as well as what is allowed and not allowed for your products, services or information.

As for the contact information you should at least put your physical location for your business and a way to contact you or a member of your company. A good way to handle that is either via a contact form or a link to your support system. By using that method you tend to cut down on subjecting that email address to unnecessary incoming email.

You can find many resources for this online by searching for each term in Google followed by template or generator such as "privacy policy template" or "terms of service generator". A product we use and recommend is AutoWebLaw.com that will create all of the documentation you need for your website.

As for the placement of these documents, it's best to have them in the footer as links at the very bottom of your webpage. Be sure to have them open as a sized pop up window so that it doesn't deter from sales or distracts the visitor by causing them to try to find how to get back to your website.

Some Other Considerations

- Domain Name Do's and Don'ts

- Simple Passwords

- Poor Web Hosting

- Advertising On Your Site

- No (Or Hard to Find) Affiliate Tools

- To Blog or Not to Blog

Biggest Website MISTAKE #46

Domain Name Do's and Don'ts

How much web traffic are you losing because of your domain name?

Let's explain…

When preparing to purchase a domain you need to think through several things in order to come up with the optimal domain name. One that takes advantage of the keywords or buzzwords your visitors would use to find your site—as well as a domain that accurately describes your product or service.

You need to be aware of words that can be commonly misspelled. There are several domain typo generators available to help you with this. If you search your favorite search engine it's generally a good idea to grab a couple of these domains if your primary domain name includes a commonly misspelled word. Some of the typo generators allow for common misspellings and common mis-keyed words—meaning words that people can easily hit the wrong key on the keyboard.

Something else to think about is if your domain name or a key part of your domain name could have a plural word. For example, one of our sites has the domain AffiliateToolPages.com. To make sure we don't lose traffic if someone doesn't type the final "s" we've also purchased AffiliateToolPage.com.

Another consideration is numbers. If you have a domain name that has a number spelled out in it then buy the domain with just the number. For instance, one of Frank's sites is ThatOneCorporation.com. He also owns That1Corporation.com, so if someone hears your domain name somewhere they will still get there with either spelling.

A final thing to think about is does your domain name spell something that you didn't intend? For instance, a domain was purchased in a hurry thinking it was a great domain for a site that was just put into place.

Web Graphics Explained is the site idea so the domain purchased was WebGraphicsExplained.com. Makes sense, right? Well, if you look closely you'll see a word that can cause you to get blocked by some email filters.

Let me point it out for you, webgraphic**SEX**plained.com.

So, there are many things to really to consider before buying your next domain.

Biggest Website
MISTAKE #47

Simple Passwords

We've seen this mistake over and over on many websites and web services that many business owners utilize. The mistake we're talking about is simplistic passwords.

Website hacking to some is a game or adventure they do to claim some sort of fame. They hack the site and then "Tag" it with their moniker or online ID to let other hackers know who got the score.

There are some things you can do to make it harder for this to happen to you. Were you aware that one of the most common passwords is actually "123456" and in some cases the password is the user's first name?

Many times we use passwords that are way too easy to guess and use the same password over and over across many sites.

So, if a hacker finds one password, chances are they will try that at other sites they can tell you use. It's not too difficult to look at the source code and see what auto responder or shopping cart service you're using. And, of course, there are many sites called "who is" sites that give you the details for who registered what domains and where they were registered.

So it's really easy to find locations to try the password they just hacked on your site.

So here are some suggestions you can use to create a stronger password.

If you can help it at all, don't use dictionary words or words that are all just alphabetical. Most sites will at least allow alphanumerics for passwords—but mix it up.

Here's an example—fishface123 would be harder than just fishface obviously, but try replacing the i with the number 1 such as f1shface. It looks similar when written but it is harder to crack and simple to remember.

Another option is to break up the syllables on such a word like f1sh2face3.

If you want to get real advanced, but still easy to remember substitute special characters for vowels. This makes an even stronger password but is still easy to remember if you use the same characters for set vowels in your passwords.

For example, fishface could become f!shf@ce. You could make it even harder by adding a significant number in the middle of the syllables or the last two digits of the current year such as f!sh09f@ce.

Just some ideas to help you become more secure when using passwords.

Biggest Website
MISTAKE #48

Poor Web Hosting

Some may not consider this a mistake. Others would consider it a catastrophe. Many may even wonder why this could cause a problem. After all, isn't every hosting company the same?

Fact is, there are a lot of things to consider when selecting web hosting. And, by not knowing what to look for in web hosting, you can easily face the lack of needed services, adequate space or even downtime with poor support.

Some things to think about when ordering hosting are things such as will you need to host more than one domain? If so, look at hosting plans that offer multiple domain accounts or what's called a reseller package. Even though you won't be reselling, this plan allows you to easily access and add multiple domains.

Another thing to look for is the amount of space available for file storage, as well as the amount of bandwidth. Obviously, if you're hosting a lot of media files such as mp3's and video, you will need more of both bandwidth and storage.

Also consider if they have an adequate amount of email accounts and database accounts. Many hosting companies allow for unlimited per domain. Others limit them. Also, you may not think you need database accounts, but actually if you are planning on adding a blog or other services chances are you will, as many of these online applications work from a database.

And speaking of blogs you will want to make sure they have Fantastico installed. This is the quickest and easiest way to get a blog installed, as well as many other online applications through the Fantastico service. Again, many times this is a free add-on. Others will either charge for it or not include it.

And finally, you want to make sure you have access to support for your hosting whether it's ticket based, phone based, or on your own. Many of the hosting companies use ticket based support. Since many questions are similar they can easily access a knowledge base for a quick reply or may even have an online knowledge base system for you to locate the answer quickly yourself.

In any case be sure you've determined what best meets your needs and plan accordingly.

Biggest Website MISTAKE #49

Advertising On Your Site

This website mistake confuses us quite a bit and we see it quite often. That is putting advertisements on your website—specifically Google AdSense and banners for other websites.

First, let's explain what Google AdSense is for those who don't know. These are mostly text ads that display either links or blocks of ads. In some cases, they even display banners. The links are placed in different areas throughout the web page.

Google AdSense was designed to show relevant ads on the website, meaning that the AdSense code knows what the topic of the page is and will display ads that match the content.

Now, some website owners think that's a good thing and, if utilized on the right type of website it is, but if you are running an online business website where you are selling a service or product you do not want Google AdSense or any other type of advertising on your pages at all.

The myth is that if you have these on your website that Google will spider your site more and by having the relevant ads on your site it will increase your relevancy and rankings for that keyword.

Truth be told, that may work. But the key fact is that not only are you giving the opportunity to your competitors to advertise on your website, you're giving your potential clients other options to click on and lead them away from your product or service and right over to your competitors. Remember, as we said these ads show "relevant" content meaning it will show ads from people advertising with the same keywords.

So not only are you defeating your purpose of keeping your website visitor on your web page(s) you are helping your competitors by giving them more places to advertise.

Biggest Website MISTAKE #50

No (Or Hard to Find) Affiliate Tools

Many times we get so wrapped up in getting the product done and the website up that we forget about all of the details to help promote the website.

What we're talking about is a website mistake many forget to do, or if they do this they don't make good use of it. That mistake would be not having or promoting your affiliate center or even having an affiliate program.

An affiliate program is where you allow people to promote your products or services for a commission. So, they get a set amount or percentage every time they make a sale for you. Think of it as your sales force, and the good thing is they don't get paid unless they make sales for you.

Sounds pretty good, doesn't it?

So this is definitely something you would want to set up and get running right away. Generally, this is something already setup in your shopping cart system. If not, there are several online applications you can use to run an affiliate program.

Once you have your program setup you want to be sure that you have an "Affiliate Center". Ideally, you would want to carry over your branding from your website or even host the affiliate center on your own site.

Be sure to include all of the tools your affiliates will need to promote your products. This would include the most common size banners, email promotions, prewritten articles, Google ads, Twitter posts, blog posts and whatever other tools you can think of.

It's good to remember that most affiliates are lazy. They want to make money but they don't want to work at it. By providing them with an affiliate tool center they can easily find what they need and quickly start earning you money.

Some good resources for banners would be 20DollarBanners. com or MiniBannersZen.com. Banners are usually one of the biggest stumbling blocks for people and these two companies can quickly get them knocked out for you.

Another program you would want to help get your affiliate center up and running is AffiliateToolGenerator.com. This is an easy to install application that you host on your website. Affiliate Tool Generator allows your affiliates to plugin their affiliate ID and push a button. Once they've done that all of the tools are now updated with their affiliate links and it's just cut and paste for them to start promoting.

So be sure to either get your affiliate (sales force) center going and start increasing sales.

Biggest Website MISTAKE #51

To Blog or Not to Blog

There are a couple of mistakes here to consider when it comes to blogs.

Now, on one hand, some would say a blog is NOT a website, but the fact is you can actually use blog software and turn it into a very functional website.

There are many templates available that will turn a WordPress blog into a functional sales letter which makes it very easy to make modifications to your website without the need for specialized software.

The first thing we want to focus on here though is the fact that many people don't use a blog at all and secondly, if they are using a blog on their website, it looks nothing like the other pages of their website.

If you're not using a blog with your website this would be the first mistake. The search engines (Google in particular) LOVE blogs. It's a good way to get traffic to your site by setting up a blog in addition to your regular sales process.

For example, you could put a blog at http://www.that1domain. com/blog then utilize the blog to publish information about your products, promo notifications, affiliate promotions and contests for THAT site. Keep it relevant, and most importantly make the blog look like the rest of your site. If this is something you can't take care of yourself you can economically have it outsourced.

If you'd like to learn more about how to best utilize blogs for your website be sure to check out the website WordPressStrategies. com to learn the basics of WordPress as well as modifying to use it as a sales letter, and/or membership site.

Bonus Mistakes

- Bonus Blunders

Bonus Blunders

There are many mistakes related to this topic alone. But, before we can talk about the mistakes, let's clarify what we mean when we are referring the word "bonus" for an online business.

By most definitions a bonus means "something extra which is given as an incentive". In most cases this has some monetary value. This is also true in your online business, but many think of a bonus as something you give your employees or yourself. In this case we are giving the bonus to our customer.

When creating our online sales process we add incentives (bonuses) to increase the value of an item which our customer is buying.

So let's talk about the mistakes that generally occur when using this strategy.

The first would seem obvious—and that would be NOT offering a bonus at all. It's not always needed but, in most cases, it does entice the potential buyer because they are getting a two for one type offer.

The second mistake would be that the bonus or bonuses that you are offering have nothing to do with the product you are selling. Imagine the confusion if you are offering an information product on "Buying Your First Home and you offer a bonus of "10 Tips to Stop Smoking Now".

This could actually confuse the buyer not help the sale. You want to think about what bonus you can offer that would accentuate the primary product you are offering.

In this example it might be something like "10 Secrets to Reduce Home Energy Costs". That would make sense because, as a first time homeowner, they are getting ready to spend a lot of money and you are giving them an added bonus of how to save money in their home.

Another mistake is not revealing the value of that bonus item. Yes, they will think "Oh cool, I get this bonus." But if the bonus has a stated value it will increase the overall value of your total offer that much more. Be sure to elevate the price of the bonus just to make it seem a better deal. Don't use your hard cost. Use terms like "real world value"; "retail value" or "sold online for $$"

Yet another mistake that is often seen when including bonuses on your website is the fact that there is no image to help your visitor visualize what that product looks like.

Many say well it's a digital product how do you show that? Easy, you create a digital representation of that item. If it's an ebook create an ecover. If it's an audio create an image with a CD or Album cover. If it's a bonus membership site show a membership card. The visual display increases the perceived value of the bonus and makes it more real to the buyer.

And that leads to our final mistake related to bonus items which is not describing what the bonus is. Just giving the title, an image and the value is nice, but don't rely on just the image to explain what they are getting. Don't leave them guessing that it's an ebook or a physical book or a CD or mp3 audio.

Give them a description such as: "This 75 page ebook reveals 10 essential secrets to reduce your utility bills with very little effort." Be sure to keep it simple though, as you don't want to deter from the sales process. Give enough information to help increase the value.

Of course, by offering digital bonuses or products this gives you a great opportunity for upselling the digital product as a physical CD for a little bit more.

Section #12

Recommended Resources

- WordPressStrategies.com
- 21WebmasterQuestions.com
- EasyWebCourse.com
- SFSBookstore.com
- WebPageSecretsRevealed.com
- 50BiggestMistakes.com
- SeminarPhotography.com
- AskDatabase.com
- Hostorix.com
- Google.com/Analytics
- AWstats.com

- RedOakCart.com
- RentaCoder.com
- GetaFreelancer.com
- AutoWebLaw.com
- 20DollarBanners.com
- MiniBannersZen.com
- AffiliateToolGenerator.com
- Kayako.com
- Speakerfulfillmentservices.com
- PayBlue.com

About the Authors

Bret Ridgway

Bret Ridgway is co-founder of Speaker Fulfillment Services, a company that works hand in hand with leading information marketers such as Alex Mandossian, Armand Morin, Perry Marshall, Ryan Deiss, Jeff Herring, Mike Stewart, Mike Koenigs, Tellman Knudson and many other well known people.

Having handled back-of-the-room sales at Internet and information marketing events for over ten years, Bret has been able to establish close working relationships with many of the top info marketers today and has been behind the scenes handling the fulfillment side of many million dollar plus new product launches.

His company has shipped out hundreds of thousands of information products for their clients over the last few years and that unique perspective has enabled Bret to see what information marketers do well – and what they don't do so well. And it's those 'what they don't do so well' factors that led to the creation of the original 50 Biggest Mistakes course—*The 50 Biggest Mistakes I See Information Marketers Make.*

Bret is author of the book *View from the Back: 101 Tips for Event Promoters Who Want to Dramatically Increase Back-of-the-Room Sales* and is a partner with Armand Morin of AM2.com and with Heather Seitz in NewsletterFormula.com

Frank Deardurff III

Frank E. Deardurff III, more well known as "That One Web Guy " is the President of That One Corporation, a Complete Web Solutions Firm located in Terre Haute, Indiana. He also serves as the CEO of Access Café Networks, Inc. In addition, Frank is co-founder of AskDataBase.com, PayBlue.com and MasterMindInABox.com

Frank comments that he has been fortunate to work with and for many top online professionals and authors some of which are Armand Morin, Alex Mandossian, Lorrie Morgan Ferrero, Mark Victor Hansen (Co-Author of Chicken Soup For The Soul), just to name a few. One of Frank's numerous projects for high profile clients, is Alex Mandossian's AccessToLeaders.com Within that campaign, Frank built sites for such notable clients as Les Brown's (AskLesBrown.com),

Brian Tracy's (JustAskBrian.com), and Stephen Covey's (AskStephenCovey.com).

A Microsoft Certified Professional since 1999, and a Certified Novell Administrator since 1996, Frank's background covers more than 25 years in Graphic Design and Technical Illustration.

Successful Internet Marketers seek to partner with Frank on projects, such as Armand Morin with PayBlue, Hostorix & CBClicks.com; Willie Crawford with Change-Web-Hosts.com and Joshua Mitchell's MasterMindInABox.com. AskDataBase.com, the World's First and ONLY search engine for survey data was also developed through a partnership with Alex Mandossian

Frank's expertise has recently found him being invited to impart his knowledge at Live Events, and dozens of Teleseminars and Webinars. Giving back to this Internet Marketing Industry, Frank also takes time to participate in multiple MasterMind groups each week.

To find more information about Frank's work, and his well designed courses that are easy to understand as well as extremely thorough in their scope, go to www.FrankDeardurff.com. Learning from Frank will set you above the curve in your Website, Strategy and Marketing education.

CLAIM YOUR EXCLUSIVE MEMBERS ACCESS

You can instantly access even more resources,
tips and bonus material **valued at $197** by visiting:

http://www.50BiggestWebsiteMistakes.com/bookbonus

When you reach that site you will be asked to register
for the special area. There is no additional charge
to gain lifetime access to this material.

By registering for the book bonus area you'll gain access to
additional resources, reviews, videos, audios and more.

Also, by registering for this exclusive area we can keep
you up to date when new information is available.

BUY A SHARE OF THE FUTURE IN YOUR COMMUNITY

These certificates make great holiday, graduation and birthday gifts that can be personalized with the recipient's name. The cost of one S.H.A.R.E. or one square foot is $54.17. The personalized certificate is suitable for framing and will state the number of shares purchased and the amount of each share, as well as the recipient's name. The home that you participate in "building" will last for many years and will continue to grow in value.

Here is a sample SHARE certificate:

THIS CERTIFIES THAT

YOUR NAME HERE

HAS INVESTED IN A HOME FOR A DESERVING FAMILY

1985-2010

TWENTY-FIVE YEARS OF BUILDING FUTURES
IN OUR COMMUNITY ONE HOME AT A TIME

1200 SQUARE FOOT HOUSE @ $65,000 = $54.17 PER SQUARE FOOT
This certificate represents a tax deductible donation. It has no cash value.

YES, I WOULD LIKE TO HELP!

*I support the work that Habitat for Humanity does and I want to be part of the excitement! As a donor, I will receive periodic updates on your construction activities but, more importantly, I know my gift will help a family in our community realize the dream of homeownership. **I would like to SHARE in your efforts against substandard housing in my community!** (Please print below)*

PLEASE SEND ME _____ SHARES at $54.17 EACH = $ $_____

In Honor Of: _____

Occasion: (Circle One)   HOLIDAY   BIRTHDAY   ANNIVERSARY

       OTHER: _____

Address of Recipient: _____

Gift From: _____ *Donor Address:* _____

Donor Email: _____

I AM ENCLOSING A CHECK FOR $ $_____ PAYABLE TO HABITAT FOR HUMANITY <u>OR</u> PLEASE CHARGE MY VISA OR MASTERCARD *(CIRCLE ONE)*

Card Number _____ Expiration Date: _____

Name as it appears on Credit Card _____ Charge Amount $ _____

Signature _____

Billing Address _____

Telephone # Day _____ Eve _____

PLEASE NOTE: Your contribution is tax-deductible to the fullest extent allowed by law.
Habitat for Humanity • P.O. Box 1443 • Newport News, VA 23601 • 757-596-5553
www.HelpHabitatforHumanity.org

CPSIA information can be obtained at www.ICGtesting.com
Printed in the USA
LVOW081647201011

251397LV00005B/12/P